For Each and Everyone

Hong Kong University Press thanks Xu Bing for writing the Press's name in his Square Word Calligraphy for the covers of its books. For further information, see p. iv.

For Each and Everyone

Catering for Individual Differences Through Learning Studies

Edited by
Lo Mun Ling, Pong Wing Yan and Pakey Chik Pui Man

香港大學出版社
HONG KONG UNIVERSITY PRESS

Hong Kong University Press
14/F Hing Wai Centre
7 Tin Wan Praya Road
Aberdeen
Hong Kong

ISBN 962 209 757 X

Secure On-line Ordering
http://www.hkupress.org

British Library Cataloguing-in-Publication Data
A catalogue record for this book is available
from the British Library.

Printed and bound by HeterMedia Services Ltd., in Hong Kong, China

Hong Kong University Press is honoured that Xu Bing, whose art explores the complex themes of language across cultures, has written the Press's name in his Square Word Calligraphy. This signals our commitment to cross-cultural thinking and the distinctive nature of our English-language books published in China.

"At first glance, Square Word Calligraphy appears to be nothing more unusual than Chinese characters, but in fact it is a new way of rendering English words in the format of a square so they resemble Chinese characters. Chinese viewers expect to be able to read Square word Calligraphy but cannot. Western viewers, however are surprised to find they can read it. Delight erupts when meaning is unexpectedly revealed."

— Britta Erickson, *The Art of Xu Bing*

Contents

Foreword

Hong Kong, like many other societies, has given serious consideration to how teachers deal with the diverse range of talents and abilities of their pupils. This concern came to the fore with the shift from elitist to mass education systems, which resulted in a far larger population of students in school and longer periods of time spent in formal education.

The Hong Kong government introduced an innovative means to help improve its schools' capacity to deal with student diversity. In 2000, it commissioned and funded five different projects, each of which was to develop, implement and disseminate a different strategy by which teachers could support the diverse needs of pupils in their classrooms. The five approaches involved, respectively, a focus on streaming pupils by abilities into subject groupings; motivation and models of learning; the development of a community of learners; the use of information technology; and, the use of variation as a guiding principle of pedagogical design to enhance learning.

This book reports on the nature and impact of the last of these projects. The project had four key features. It developed a form of "Learning Studies" which built upon the Japanese tradition of "Lesson Studies." Secondly, it used Variation Theory developed by Marton and his colleagues (1997, 1998) as its theoretical underpinning. Thirdly, it viewed pupil diversity as a positive feature of schooling and not as a problem, such that catering for diversity was viewed primarily as a matter of pedagogy to be addressed in the act of teaching. Finally, the strategy reported in this volume was developed with teachers through a process which was grounded in the reality of classrooms. What resulted was not a set of propositions developed solely from a theoretical framework, but rather a means to strongly empower teachers to work together and improve their pedagogy.

The impact of the project is also reported in this volume. It is evident from the data and from speaking to those who have been involved with the project that it has transformed not only the pedagogy in many schools, but also created amongst many teachers a process which has facilitated both their ongoing professional growth and improved the culture of their schools. It has rekindled in teachers the belief that all children are capable of learning once their learning needs and the object of learning for any particular lesson are clearly identified, especially those children who have hitherto been considered to have low ability. The work reported in this volume deserves to be given close attention by teachers and all those concerned with educating the next generation of citizens.

Paul Morris
President
The Hong Kong Institute of Education

Acknowledgements

We are very grateful to the Curriculum Development Institute of the Education and Manpower Bureau, the Hong Kong Special Administrative Region, for its generous support and encouragement, which made this project possible.

During the course of this study, we worked with two primary schools and carried out twenty-nine Learning Studies on various topics in mathematics, Chinese language, general studies, and English language. We would like to express our sincerest gratitude to the school heads and teachers who gave so willingly their time. Their generosity in facilitating the studies is deeply appreciated. We owe our special thanks to the teachers and students who agreed to let us observe and record their teaching and learning, and shared their experiences with us in interviews. Without their cooperation and support, completion of this study would not have been possible.

Lo Mun Ling
on behalf of the research team

RESEARCH TEAM

Principal Investigators

Dr LO Mun Ling (September 2000–February 2004)
Dr PONG Wing Yan (September 2001–February 2004)

Consultant

Professor Ference MARTON (September 2000–February 2004)

Team Members (in alphabetical order)

Dr KO Po Yuk (September 2000–February 2004)
Dr LEUNG Yuk Lun Allen (September 2001–February 2004)
Ms LO-FU Yin Wah Priscilla (September 2001–February 2004)
Ms NG Fung Ping Dorothy (September 2000–February 2004)
Dr PANG Ming Fai (September 2000–February 2004)
Dr PONG Wing Yan (September 2000–August 2001)

Officer of Curriculum Development Institute

Ms WONG Sau Yim Josephine (September 2000–February 2004)

Research Staff (in alphabetical order)

Ms CHAN Sau Shan Fion (F/T, R.A. I, September 2001–August 2002)
Ms CHIK Pui Man Pakey (F/T, S.R.A., September 2000–February 2004)
Ms LI Nga Sze Sabrina (F/T, R.A. I, September 2002–August 2003)
Mr KWOK Wing Yin (P/T, R.A. I, September 2001–July 2003;
    F/T, S.R.A, August 2003)
Ms TANG Nga Chi (F/T, R.A. I, August 2001–August 2002)

1

Predominant Explanations of Individual Differences and Methods of Handling These Differences

LO Mun Ling and PONG Wing Yan

Introduction

In 2000, the Curriculum Development Institute in Hong Kong initiated research with an aim to find ways to cater for individual differences in students attending mainstream schools in Hong Kong. Our research team, comprising twelve researchers and a consultant from Göteborg University, was one of five independent teams that worked on the project. The first task that we faced was to create a working definition of "individual differences," with the understanding that the term might mean very different things to different people and as a result would lead to varying ways of addressing the issue. The initial discussion focused on why people were so concerned about individual differences. We asked, "In a pluralistic society, don't we need people with various abilities, temperaments, and interests, who are able to contribute to, and take up, diverse roles in society? Indeed, is the world not a more interesting place when people are different from what it would be otherwise?" We tried to grapple with the concerns of educators and the government, to understand why "individual differences" is such a great issue.

In Hong Kong as in other places, students are put together in schools and in classrooms. They are often expected to learn at the same rate and achieve the same learning outcomes through engaging in the same activities. However, in practice it is observed that some students learn more effectively or faster than others, and this is often attributed to individual differences. As it is perceived that, within the same classroom, students learning at different rates and achieving at different levels is problematic, the fact that students differ is also regarded as problematic and as something that must be dealt with in one way or another.

Students' success and failure at school is often explained either by the individual differences between learners in their innate abilities or motivation, or by the appropriate or inappropriate application of teaching arrangements that the teachers use (e.g., see Entwistle, 1984). Each of these explanations is associated with certain viewpoints on how the school or the teacher should handle the problem or remedy the situation. These are also the most predominant views held by teachers, teacher educators, and policy makers in Hong Kong.

In the space below, we explain why these views, though each has its own merits, are rather unproductive in helping children to achieve mastery of basic competences. Neither do they provide adequate help to teachers in dealing with the issue of individual differences within the constraints that they face.

However, the reader must be cautioned that, throughout our discussion, we refer to children within the range of "normal" abilities; that is, they are neither mentally impaired nor exceptionally gifted to the extent that they cannot benefit from an inclusive education.

Difference in learning outcomes and difference in ability

It is often observed that some pupils learn more quickly or more easily than others. An easy explanation of such a fact is that they are born with different innate abilities. The popularity of such a viewpoint is evident by the abundance of "check your own IQ" type publications available in local bookstores. It is believed that, because children are pre-wired with relatively stable but different abilities, the way to cater for individual differences is to identify and classify children into groups according to such abilities, and then teach them only those things they are capable of learning. This appears to employ the metaphor that children are different kinds of vessel with varying capacities. As you cannot pour one litre of water into a 500 ml vessel, you should try to fill it up only with 500 ml of water, or it will overflow. So, different strategies have evolved to match the input to the child's assumed capacity, including streaming, banding, the use of graded worksheets and differentiated curricula, and so forth. Whereas psychologists are divided on the question of whether there exists a general intellectual ability, whether such an ability (if it exists) may change significantly over time, or whether intelligence is in fact multiple rather than singular (Gardner, 1984), we would argue that, whatever the merits of the argument or usefulness of associated teaching arrangements suggested, there are two inherent problems associated with these viewpoints.

First, children classified as having lower abilities are deprived of the opportunity of learning that which they are perceived to be "unable to learn." This raises a question of social equity regarding whether children are being treated fairly. Moreover, the gap between the "more-able" and "less-able" students will be widened, thus aggravating the problem and increasing the need to cater for student diversity. Second, children who are labelled low ability are often able to surprise us by learning seemingly difficult things. For example, despite differences in rate of learning, most young children will succeed in learning to speak their mother tongue with fluency by the age of five. For very specific abilities, such as memory and retention, many children of the same age may exhibit superior ability by demonstrating that they have excellent recall of their friends' birthdays, telephone numbers, and even pieces of song lyrics while, at the same time, showing great difficulties in recalling the facts stated in the textbook, which they committed to memory through repetition.

Measures such as streaming, banding, and curriculum setting, which reduce the possible diversity experienced in class, may help to bring about teacher confidence or encourage teachers to focus on teaching methods that are tailored to individual groups. However, apart from the two problems described above, educational research is replete with evidence that numerous deviant behaviours are, in fact, due to the effects of labelling which are not actually substantiated by rigorous ability measurements. Children in so-called "ability groups" often perform to teachers' expectations rather than to their real abilities. It has also been shown that students do pick up cues from the behaviours of teachers regarding their abilities, when they are treated differentially. This in turn affects how they account for their own successes and failures in schoolwork. Attribution of failure to lack of ability often leads to resignation and predictions of more failure (e.g., Werner, 1980). The danger of constructing a self-fulfilling prophecy about "ability" thus cannot be understated.

Difference in learning outcomes and difference in motivation

In educational research, the effects of pupil motivation on school attainment have been widely studied. Some researchers argue that the findings suggest that, for all ages and at all ability levels, pupils with higher motivation perform better than those with lower motivation (e.g., Solomon and Kendall, 1979).

Theories regarding motivation are numerous and varied. The traditional behaviourist model explains motivation according to reinforcements experienced through stimulus-response reactions but fails to account for the observation that most teachers have, that students subjected to similar "reinforcement" contingencies could exhibit vastly different levels of persistence or patience in dealing with the same task.

Cognitive theories of motivation tend to focus on the possible internal events that may give rise to the differences in engagement in tasks. Apart from the same question regarding whether motivation is a personal trait, or if it is, whether it is a stable one, the general view nowadays is that there could be different types of motivation or motivational style, and hence the distinction between extrinsic and intrinsic motivation. If extrinsic motivation is brought about by the teacher using strategies like games, praise, rewards, and interesting activities, it may well help some students learn more efficiently, especially young children who often lack sustained concentration on one object.

One reason for a child's poor learning outcome may therefore be due to his or her not paying attention to what the teacher says, and so the child misses some important pieces of information. If children are motivated by what they are doing, they will pay more attention to it, be willing to spend more time on it, and so learn more effectively. This belief was widely held in the heyday of behaviourism, when learning was taken as a set of stimulus-response reactions. Though the behaviourist model is no longer thought to be adequate in explaining complex learning, it has been consistently applied to areas in which training is conducted through repetitive practice. For example, when a child is motivated to do sums, driven by an extrinsic reward, eventually, the child will master the skills of doing sums accurately and swiftly. However, one must be cautious in using extrinsic motivational measures such as teachers' sanctioning activities (e.g., praise and the show of displeasure, or rewards such as a degree qualification). They may induce desired student behaviour more effectively but do not guarantee deep understanding, or that "students will acquire the kinds of knowledge that will support new learning" (Bransford et al., 2002, 24). A typical example is the finding that even university students of physics did not really understand the physics that they learnt (Clement, 1982, 1983; Gardner, 1991, 152–5).

As far as intrinsic motivation is concerned, it is contextually and content bound. It is often observed that the same child who is described as being motivated in learning one thing may not show much or any interest in learning another thing within the same school curriculum or under the same teacher. Thus we cannot talk about motivation without referring to what is being learnt and how it is experienced by the learner — the object of learning (the concept of the "object of learning" is more fully explored in Chapter 2). Although some cognitive scientists have expressed the view that psychologists' accounts of motivation in learning can be nothing more than "warmed-over common sense" (Bereiter and Scardamalia, 1993, 101), we would at least agree that children are generally unable to acquire the sort of "intrinsic motivation" required to bring about a long-term engagement with the subject matter.

The argument about the high value of intrinsic motivation on learning, achievement, and creativity is often explained by increased effort and engagement due to the learner's experience of sustained pleasure or "flow" (Csikszentmihayi, 1988). The difficulty, however, is that schooling is structured in such a way that most children do not experience the teacher's teaching objectives as their immediate or felt needs. Young children are typically not interested in long hauls, as Skemp (1971) argued about the case of mathematics learning:

> [Mathematics] is widely known to be an essential tool for science, technology, and commerce; and for entry to many professions. These are goals which motivate many adults to mathematics; but they are too remote to be applicable to the early years of school, when we first begin mathematics. (1971, 132)

Even for learners with high intrinsic motivation, there is no guarantee that deep learning will result. Highly motivated scientists may have to struggle for years before they learn and see what is critical in their study, and come to a breakthrough in their research, as the well-known story of how Madam Curie discovered radon illustrates. Entwistle (1984), in summarizing many studies in psychology and educational psychology on intelligence, motivation, and study skills, came to the conclusion that such research had made relatively little impact on helping students to learn better. He blamed such researchers for taking only their own perspective and ignoring the students' perspective:

> These researchers continued … implicitly or explicitly to blame the students for low levels of academic attainment. Thus failure is explained away as the result of low ability or lack of organization or application. (p. 12)

To truly access the learners' perspective, we believe we have to

> … ask learners what their experiences are like, watch what they do, observe what they learn and what makes them learn, analyse what learning is for them. (Marton and Booth, 1997, 16)

Furthermore, in order for children to experience "flow," or the joy of learning, they must be able to experience the sense of curiosity and excitement about a subject. Thus, it is not possible to induce intrinsic motivation in students without first studying very carefully why the intended learning is relevant to the students, how it can be made easy to understand, accessible, and yet without loss of depth. Teachers have the responsibility of pointing the way and structuring student experiences to enable them to learn, instead of just leaving it to chance.

The above, of course, is not an effort to negate the importance of motivation but to point out that efforts to bring about intrinsic motivation may have only limited effectiveness without due consideration given to what is to be learnt and how it is experienced by the learner. We would also like to reiterate that extrinsic motivational measures such as teachers' sanctioning activities (e.g., praise and the show of displeasure) may produce some desired pupil behaviours but, as many experienced teachers would agree, it guarantees no deep understanding or learning unless the way the subject matter is dealt with and how it relates to the learners are seriously taken into account.

Difference in learning outcomes and difference in teaching arrangement

More recently, research on student learning has been moving away from seeing learning as mainly an individual construction of knowledge to emphasizing the social and cultural character of learning (Resnick, Levine and Teasley, 1991; Mercer, 2000). Learning, as these researchers argue, is seen as most effective when the learner is immersed in a community of practitioners such as in an apprenticeship arrangement (Lave, 1996), in which human artefacts, rather than just the brainpower of the learner alone, contribute to the learning outcome. Learning is therefore not just in the head but distributed in the environment. Although admitting that school knowledge is inevitably institutional and social in nature, they consider school learning the most alienated and ineffective form of learning, because the learning activity takes place in an unauthentic environment where the learning outputs are increasingly mental (rather than physical) in nature, and they are most unlikely to be anything immediately useful (Säljö, 1996). According to this view, school learning is almost destined to fail.

Accompanying such a shift in the conception of learning is the focus on the social interactions in the process of learning, as well as the stress on the need to create teaching arrangements that promote teacher-student interactions. There is an unprecedented emphasis on the importance of artefacts, context, set-up work, and grouping arrangements to facilitate the interaction between the learners as well as with the environment.

The presence of interactions, in our view, is a necessary but not sufficient condition for learning. Although we have observed instances of children learning better in authentic situations where there are social interactions and ample sharing of life experiences, it is hard to imagine that interactions alone will guarantee the achievement of the learning outcomes intended by the teacher in school. Emphasis on interactions can move us away from the directional nature of school teaching, and, as a result, the purpose of learning may become opaque, and the criteria used by the teacher in judging learning success may not be understood. The chance that the learner will learn what is expected of him or her is perhaps equally as great as that of the learner learning something he or she is not expected to learn.

More seriously, the fervour of "situated learning" and "social interactions" has created a kind of unfortunate misunderstanding among some practitioners. There is a belief that, once students form groups and participate in communal activities, learning will naturally take place. Concerning the issue of individual differences, there has been a view that the diversity among the members of a group will create, in an automatic manner, new learning experiences leading to knowledge construction.

What we wish to point out is that learning in school usually begins from a situation in which the learners do not actually know what they do not know. This makes it impossible for the learner to play a part in setting the criteria for judging success. Educational research is replete with studies which show the huge gap between what Gardner and others refer to as "intuitive knowledge" that children bring with them to school and "school knowledge" that is intended for them (e.g., Gardner, 1991). The knowledge the teacher wishes to develop is often remote from the student's everyday experience. For example, children experience the sun rising in the east and setting in the west, but in school they are taught that this "phenomenon" is caused by the rotation of the earth itself. The rotation of the earth is not something that children can easily experience, but the rising and setting of the sun is "real" to their everyday encounter.

In ideal "situated learning," the learner is put among the "knowers," so that the learner learns intimately through modelling, interacting, and following the instructions of the "knowers." For example, in an immersion programme, a child who cannot speak English is put among native speakers of English, so the child learns through everyday interactions with these native speakers and acquires the language. However, it must be considered that, in school, this rarely occurs. In most cases, the teacher is the only "knower" in the classroom. By relying on small-group interactions, there is always the danger that children are deprived of the opportunity of being taught by a teacher. More seriously, they may be misled by one or other of their peers who take the role of "teacher" in the group.

It is thus dangerous to argue that the existence of individual differences within a group, rather than the deliberate guiding effort of the teacher, provides the impetus for learning. Although we approve of the rather positive disposition (as opposed to the generally negative view) towards individual differences, we hasten to add that the optimism that individual differences will automatically work for learning is completely unjustified and mislaid. Our view is that individual differences are a double-edged sword, which can facilitate learning when they are handled by a teacher who is able to harness them. When left to run its own course, individual differences can be a natural reinforcer for the "intuitive" knowledge we described above, adding difficulties to the pursuit of learning.

The rise of "situated learning" and "social interaction" theories has also added fuel to the debate regarding the effectiveness of various teaching arrangements, such as whole-class teaching versus individualized instruction, group discussion versus seatwork, small class versus large class, the use of technology in teaching versus the simple use of chalk and board, as if questions such as the guiding role of the teacher, the content of teaching (that is, what is to be taught) or the intention of the teacher and students involved and the actual learning outcomes (for example, whether students conduct the learning act to satisfy a drive for knowledge or if they are simply fulfilling their study requirements) are insignificant or of lesser importance.

To us, it is inconceivable that there is a best way of teaching anything, and it would be grossly inappropriate to make sweeping statements regarding the effectiveness of particular teaching arrangements (such as whole-class teaching versus individualized instruction, group discussions versus seatwork, small class versus large class, etc.) without making reference to what is intended to be learnt.

Summary

We accept that the school is a social institution that must have a prescribed curriculum and a set of expected learning outcomes for each grade level. This is to ensure that students will acquire basic competences in preparation for their future participation in a modern society. We also accept that, because of resource constraints, teaching in school must take place in groups and in a place called the "classroom." However, we believe that it is not necessary to view "individual differences" as problematic.

In this chapter, we reviewed a number of perspectives on individual differences. We have also explained why we believe the ways they propose for dealing with the issue would not be very useful for practicing teachers. In the next chapter, we present the view of our research team and how we propose to deal with the issue.

2

Catering for Individual Differences: Building on Variation

LO Mun Ling and PONG Wing Yan

Introduction

Instead of seeing the learner as a set of stimulus-response reactions, a bundle of nerves, or a number on the score sheet of a test or an inventory, some educators believe that we should be looking at the issue from a more humanistic perspective that enables us to explain learning from the possible "experiences" that the student has gone through in the process of learning. This approach of studying learning, though still not favoured by most psychologists (probably due to the lack of experimental control), is increasingly favoured in the field of education. In this book, we present a view of learning that stems from a humanistic interest and, as a result, addresses learning from a pedagogical perspective.

In this chapter, we first explain our view of individual differences. We then illustrate how we understand learning, using a conceptual framework that is based on the Theory of Variation (Marton and Booth, 1997). We then put forth a theory of pedagogy which is premised on our view of teaching and learning; and finally, we explain how such a pedagogy can be used to cater for individual differences.

Difference in learning outcomes and difference in the way of seeing the same thing

In the past three decades, there has been an increasing interest in educational research on work related to students' understanding of science concepts and theories. What emerged is a conclusion that students do bring their own ideas and beliefs about the world (especially about natural phenomena) into the classroom. These ideas and beliefs, which are often in conflict with the science concepts that the teacher tries to teach, have been a major obstacle to learning. Based on a similar interest, a group of researchers, led by Professor Ference Marton of Göteborg University, Sweden, developed a research perspective known as "phenomenography." Its main research programme was to explore and describe the differences in how people understood, experienced, or thought about a particular phenomenon or an aspect of the world. Based on a large number of studies, they arrived at an important conclusion; that is, people often experience the same phenomenon in qualitatively different ways. However, when these differences are rigorously examined, they are always limited in number (Marton, 1977). A frequently quoted example is Säljö's (1982) study on how people come to understand or experience a text. In the study, the researcher asked a group of university students to read a passage on the topic of learning, and then he probed how they understood what they had read. What he found was that, although these students were reading the same text, they actually derived different meanings from it. Eventually, two distinct ways of understanding the text were identified. Firstly, some students saw the text as having a sequential structure with different perspectives of learning being described but bearing no relationship to each other. The second view, as demonstrated by another group of students, was that the text contained a main theme (the forms of learning), illustrated by a number of sub-themes (different perspectives of learning). This group of students saw the text as having a hierarchical structure with clear relationships between the sub-themes and the main theme. Säljö also found that the students who understood the text in the hierarchical way were better able to grasp the main idea of the text than those who understood the text in the sequential way, in the sense that the former group of students demonstrated a more organized and meaningful way of understanding.

Seen from this light, it is not difficult to understand why learning outcomes often vary within a group of students. In fact, variations in learning outcome should be the norm rather than the exception, because, for the same learning material or teaching act, students might understand the material or experience the teaching act in different ways. For example, while some students may not see any relationship among the different parts of the teacher's presentation, others may understand the same presentation as containing a theme with subsuming or related parts. For the same act of teaching, some students may see it as the transmission of factual knowledge that can be retained by regurgitation, but others may see it as challenging their existing understanding and requiring deep reflection in order to fully comprehend what has been espoused.

Studies from the phenomenographic tradition have repeatedly provided a similar conclusion: although people do have qualitatively different understandings of a certain object, event, or phenomenon, one often assumes that others understand the object, event, or phenomenon in exactly the same way as one does. In teaching, it is only too easy for teachers to assume that their students will understand their teaching only in the way that they intend. The first step to improving teaching is, therefore, for the teacher to recognize that the students may understand what he or she intends to teach in different ways, thus achieving different learning outcomes. It follows that the central task of teaching would be, first, to find out what these different ways of understanding are and, second, to consider how teaching should be structured to enable students to see what is taught in the intended way.

Pong and Morris (2002), in summarizing the findings of a number of meta-analyses on the effects of curriculum reforms on student achievements, also point out that some innovations, including those focusing on teaching styles or strategies, are of peripheral significance in exerting influence on student learning, and the crux actually lies in how a specific content of learning is made available to students. In Marton and Tsui (2004), a set of studies are used to illustrate that the way the specific content of learning is dealt with has a significant effect on student learning. These studies show empirically what might seem self-evident: it is more likely that students learn when it is possible for them to learn than when it is not. That is, it matters how the teacher structures the lesson to enable the students to see in specific ways what is to be learnt. Seen from this light, we think that teaching arrangements can only be judged by how the learning of *something* is being made possible. In other words, attention must be paid to what is to be learnt.

We believe that what prevents students from fully understanding their lesson in school is not primarily their lack of ability or the failure of teachers to arrange the classroom in certain ways (e.g., pair work, group work) but mainly students' incomplete ways of understanding what is to be learnt in the lesson. This may be caused by a number of reasons:

a. Students bring with them "intuitive" ways of understanding, which may become obstacles to new ways of understanding when the two seem to be in conflict.
b. Students fail to focus on all the critical aspects of what is to be learnt.
c. Students have not been exposed to suitable learning experiences in the lesson that would have enabled them to learn.

For example, when a group of young children was asked to draw what they meant by the Earth being round, some representations showed the Earth as a disc, others as a hemisphere (e.g., Nussbaum, 1985; Vosniadou and Brewer, 1987, 1990, 1992, 1993).

Common to all these representations is the conception that people must stay on top of the Earth and not be hanging upside down. Thus, what presents itself as an obstacle to learning, in this case, is the gravitational force that keeps people on the surface of the Earth without falling off into space, even when they are seen to be upside down. The concept of gravitational force is therefore critical to making a correct interpretation of "the Earth is round." In other

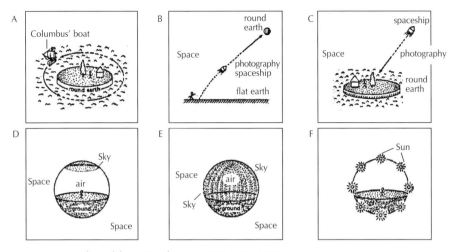

(Diagrams adapted from Nussbaum, 1985, 179, 182)

words, "gravitational force" is a "critical aspect" required to achieve the correct understanding (a detailed discussion of the idea of "critical aspect" is provided on p. 16).

One cannot make the learner discern a certain critical aspect (such as "gravitational force") by simply pointing it out. Learners must discern and make sense of what they discern for themselves. The following episode from our own research is revealing. A lesson was taught by a teacher to a Primary 3 class on the topic of the three states of water. The teacher first put some ice into a zipped plastic bag, and then she placed the bag of ice inside a metal can. Pointing to the water droplets forming on the surface of the can, the teacher asked the children where these water droplets came from. A discussion followed. In the end, the teacher helped the students to arrive at the conclusion that the water droplets came from air, as air contained water vapour that condensed on the cold surface of the metal can. After the lesson, a researcher interviewed a student about what she had learnt:

Student A:	Ms W said that water will leak from the bag of ice when it is cold. It really did, the water made my hands wet …
Interviewer:	Did the water leak from the bag of ice? But it was in a zipped plastic bag!
Student A:	… It's like the bottle of drink I brought this morning; it was cold, and it leaked.
Interviewer:	Let me ask you a question: is there water vapour in air?
Student A:	No … Yes.
Interviewer:	Why did you say "no" in the first place?
Student A:	Because I remembered what Ms W said.
Interviewer:	Don't try to recall from memory … . Think on your own. Is there water vapour in air?

Student A: No ... I cannot see any ...
Interviewer: Now, let me ask you again. Is there water vapour in air?
Student A: (Shaking her head firmly) No.
Interviewer: You said "no." Why?
Student A: Water vapour will vanish, and it will change back to air.

Although Student A, as a "good student," could repeat what the teacher told her in class, she had difficulty accepting the fact that the water droplets came from air. The notion that there is water vapour in air is simply not supported by her daily experience. This is another example of the difference in ways of seeing that needs to be dealt with. The way of seeing that arises from intuitive understanding stands in the way of the kind of understanding that schools intend to cultivate. Children do not learn by being told. Thus, effective teaching requires the elicitation of students' pre-existing understanding, and opportunities must be provided to students to build on their initial understanding. Students' preconceptions must be challenged and directly addressed, for them to be transformed or expanded (Bransford et al., 2002).

This is not to deny that children may be born with different abilities, and that some will therefore achieve far more or better than others. As teachers, there is nothing we can do about the differences in inherent aptitudes. We cannot make children naturally more able. But we believe that the range of abilities among children studying in mainstream schools should not hinder these children from learning what is intended in the school curriculum. Furthermore, a child has a right to reach her or his full potential. Therefore, in catering for individual differences, our focus is not on the variation in abilities; rather, we focus on the variation in learning outcomes. We believe that, if we can help students to acquire more powerful ways of seeing, it will be more likely that they are able to achieve the intended learning outcomes.

In any given lesson, there will be certain capabilities, e.g., understanding of a certain subject content and/or skill that the teacher intends to nurture. These are the intended learning outcomes, and they need to be clearly identified, because some are more important and worthwhile than others. There are also certain basic, core elements that everyone should learn and master, if one is to continue to learn and develop. These are sometimes defined as basic competences. Unfortunately, in schools, very little attention has been paid to these core elements. Moreover, for every worthwhile learning outcome that we can identify, there are some critical aspects that can be further identified and communicated. We believe that how the critical aspects are identified is not simply a matter of analysing and distilling them from the knowledge base of the subject disciplines. They have to be pinpointed from studying the interaction of the students with the subjects, and in the cultural context that the students are situated. These critical aspects may also vary according to the age, maturity, and experience of the students.

Our point of departure is that, by catering for individual differences, we mean that we are helping every child to learn what is worthwhile, essential, and reasonable to learn, so that every child can proceed in schooling. Next, we illustrate with examples our view of teaching and learning and discuss our approach to handling individual differences in the classroom.

Our view of teaching and learning

A number of concepts are pertinent in understanding our view of teaching and learning: object of learning, critical aspects, the structure of awareness, discernment, and variation. Since we believe that learning involves an interaction between the learner and what is to be learnt, we start by explaining the concept of the "object of learning."

The object of learning

The concept of the "object of learning" is derived from Brentano's principle of "intentionality" (1874). The concept of intentionality has nothing to do with intentions but rather with the observation that all mental acts are *directed* towards an object. Intentionality is concerned with the directedness of the mind. The key point is that one cannot simply experience without experiencing something. Similarly, one cannot think without thinking about something, nor can one learn without learning something. To talk about the learning act or behaviour alone would be hollow, if we do not at the same time make references to that which is learnt. Contrary to the belief of some educational theorists, therefore, we believe that one simply cannot develop thinking in isolation from the objects of thought. Learning is always the learning of something, and we cannot talk about learning without paying attention to what is being learnt.

We understand that, to most readers, the word "object" usually means "a visible or tangible thing." This is such a strong association that it is difficult to shift immediately to another dictionary meaning ("the end towards which effort is directed" or "an aim, goal or intention"). In our use of the term "object of learning," we take the latter meaning, i.e., the end towards which the learning activity is directed and how it is made sense of by the learner. Therefore, we take objects of learning as capabilities; they are not confined to the understanding of concepts or theories, but they can also be associated with skills, attitudes, or values. Thus, an object of learning has two aspects: a general aspect and a specific aspect. The general aspect has to do with the capabilities we wish to nurture in the students, and the specific aspect with the subject matter we are dealing with and upon which the capabilities are being built or exercised.

In choosing an "object of learning," one cannot simply make reference to a set of topics or concepts and their places within the content or structure of an academic discipline, such as mathematics. Rather, the rationale for learning a certain concept must be found within the encounters between the learners and what is to be learnt, the value of which is derived from how such experiences open up opportunities for the learners to understand the world around them. For example, instead of taking the learning of "fractions" as a matter of course in the primary curriculum, we should ask stringent questions about the enabling functions that the learning of fractions brings for the learners in making sense of their environment. According to Marton and Booth (1997), when someone encounters a situation, some aspects appear to be more relevant to him or her than other aspects, and so the situation acquires a relevance structure: "the person's experience of what the situation calls for, what it demands" (p. 143). Since how one understands the situation depends on what critical aspects one attends to, the relevance structure of the situation largely determines the learning that takes place. Thus, if teachers are not being mindful of why students are learning what they are learning, it will be difficult for them to achieve deep learning outcomes.

Consequently, we should not simply cover the syllabus/curriculum prescribed without asking stringent questions like: Is the teaching of this topic worthwhile? How is it related to the goal of education? What capabilities do we wish to nurture in the students? What are the difficulties that my students will encounter when learning this topic? What must they have learnt before they can acquire this particular concept/skill? How is this topic related to the rest of the topics that are to be taught later in the year?

We further differentiate three types of object of learning: the "intended" object of learning, the "enacted" object of learning, and the "lived" object of learning (Marton, Runesson and Tsui, 2004). By having the two terms "enacted" and "lived" object of learning, we formally acknowledge the fact that students do not always learn what is intended. The enacted object of learning is the result of the teachers' enactment during the lesson, which makes it possible for the students to learn certain things; but it may equally well be possible, because of the dynamic situation of the classroom, that the intended object of learning and the enacted object of learning do not overlap. What a student actually learns depends on what he or she experienced, i.e., the lived object of learning. Each student may experience the same situation in different ways; thus the lived object of learning will be different for different individuals. That is, even when the teacher has made it possible for the students to learn certain things, we cannot assume that the students would experience them in the same way as intended and thus learn.

Critical aspects

Once we have defined the object of learning, we have to identify the critical aspects of the object of learning, in other words, what is critical in order for students to acquire the intended capability. As mentioned earlier, how we understand an object or a phenomenon depends on what critical aspects we focus on. In order for students to understand the subject matter under study in the way intended, teachers must be clear about what critical aspects needed to be discerned. This will firstly require them to have sound knowledge of the progress of inquiry, the terms of discourse, the relationship between information and the concepts that help organize that information in the discipline, in order to define the different aspects that should be learnt with respect to the object of learning. Secondly, among all the aspects, teachers should be able to identify those which are critical because they cause difficulty for the students in the process of learning. Some critical aspects are more easily discerned than others. Those aspects that are not easily discerned by the teacher often present themselves as obstacles to students' learning.

The reason why it may not be easy for teachers to identify the critical aspects that cause students difficulty is that teachers themselves often do not find these aspects difficult to discern, and may thus take them for granted. They are unable to highlight these aspects in their teaching because they are not even aware of them. As a result, a learning gap is left unattended. Those students who happen to be able to discern these aspects will come to a better understanding of the topic and are considered to be more able students by the teachers. Those who do not discern these aspects are left puzzled. These students cannot progress in their learning, not because they lack ability, but because they have missed some pieces of information that are very important. Consider the following question: What is the fraction represented by the shaded part?

Those students who take the unit as two squares will give the answer

14/16, because they see the two squares as being divided into sixteen portions, each portion being 1/16 of the whole, and there are altogether fourteen such portions. In contrast, those students who take the unit as one square will give the answer 14/8, since they see each square as being divided into eight portions, each portion being 1/8 of a square, and there are fourteen of them. Both answers are, in fact, correct if the units are clearly specified. However, if the teacher had in mind the question 8/8 + 6/8 and is using the diagram as an illustration, then the only acceptable answer would be 14/8, as one square has been taken for granted to be the unit. Students who see the unit as two squares and hence give the answer as 14/16 are very quickly given the feedback that their logic is wrong and that they are "less able" at learning mathematics. If the teacher wants to help students learn, he or she must first recognize the students' logic and how this logic may hinder their learning, and then address it accordingly. The recognition of what constitutes difficulties for the students in learning, however, requires the knowledge of what is critical for the learning. In this case, being able to focus on the "unit" is critical for the learning of fractions in mathematics to take place (Lamon, 1999). In other words, "unit" should be taken as a *critical aspect* for the understanding of fractions.

Another example is the study of astronomical phenomena in the primary general studies curriculum. The students are expected to learn topics like the four seasons, solar and lunar eclipses, tides, Earth, the Sun, the Moon, as well as the rotation and revolution of the Moon and Earth. Without carefully analysing what the object of learning should be, what the critical aspects are, and how these are related, teachers often feel that they are confronted with, and have to conform to, a curriculum which matches the description by Bransford et al. (2002) as failing to support learning with understanding because they "present too many disconnected facts in too short a time — the mile wide, inch deep problem" (p. 24). To help students learn these topics, the teacher must first be able to understand why this topic would be difficult for students to learn. The geocentric perspective is more akin to students' intuitive understanding, because they can only see the movements of the Moon and the Sun but not that of Earth, as they are standing on it. The teaching of these topics in fact requires students to change from taking a geocentric perspective to taking a heliocentric perspective. The object of learning here would be an understanding of the part of the solar system of which the Sun, the Earth, and the Moon are parts. Concepts like gravitational force and how it operates between these celestial bodies resulting in rotation and revolution are critical aspects to the understanding of the object of learning. Once students can fully grasp these concepts, they can easily explain and deduce for themselves natural events or phenomena like the different phases of the Moon, solar eclipse, lunar eclipse, as well as why there are four seasons on Earth.

The structure of awareness

Having identified the object of learning and its associated critical aspects, how are we going to help the students to learn them? As we have illustrated with the example of learning the three states of water (see pp. 12–3 above), students do not learn by just *being told.* Rather, the way in which the learner comes to understand a particular phenomenon has to do with his or her *awareness* — the totality of a person's experience of the specified situation.

Human awareness has a structure. Since we cannot be simultaneously aware of everything at the same time, some objects or aspects will come to the fore of our awareness and be focused on, while those not focused on will recede into the background (Miller, 1956; Marton and Booth, 1997). For example, while you are reading this sentence, you are focusing on this sentence and its meaning. The sentence comes to the fore of your awareness. You are still aware of the rest of the text, but only as letters on the page. They have receded into the background. In your awareness, there are also other things. For example, you are still aware that you will be having dinner with your family in the evening, or that you need to get a certain assignment finished. However, they will remain in the background unless they are suddenly mentioned, as now. This is similar to a figure and ground relationship. When something comes to the forefront of your awareness, it is discerned from the background and is in your focal awareness. Learning is discerning something which has not been noticed or discerned by the learner, so that it becomes the figure instead of the background.

Every object has many aspects. For example, if you look at a hand, you may notice that there are five fingers, there are lines on the hand and prints on the fingers, etc. Depending on the features being discerned, we would have different understandings of the hand. The reverse is also true. Depending on how we aim to understand the hand, we need to focus on different aspects. If the purpose of looking at the hand is to read the fortune, then the pattern of lines on the palm is a critical aspect. If a criminologist is looking at the hand as a source of identification of a person, the fingerprint is a critical aspect. If an artist is looking at the same hand, the space that the fingers make when curved and the sense of power expressed by the shape become critical aspects. Thus, although a hand has many aspects, certain aspects are critical for a specific way of seeing.

If we wish to teach a child what a telephone is, we must help the child to focus on the critical aspects that make the object a telephone. Children who think that a mobile phone *is not* a telephone, or that a toy telephone *is* a telephone have partial or incomplete understanding of telephones, because they fail to focus on one of the critical aspects of a telephone — its functional aspect. That is, it is a tool for communication. Instead, they focus on the external features or parts that make up a telephone.

In order to help children learn, teachers must first identify the critical aspects and then help their students focus on these critical aspects at the same time, in order to bring about an intended way of understanding. Failing to discern a critical aspect may lead to obstacles in learning. Children's understanding of the fact that the Earth is round, mentioned earlier in this chapter, is a good example. Children are quite ready to regurgitate the facts that their teachers have told them. However, when these facts do not fit in with their own logic, the children stick to their own ways of seeing things.

Discernment and variation

Learning by being able to focus on the critical aspects, as Bowden and Marton (1998) argue, is regarded as a function of *discernment* that presupposes an experienced *variation* in those aspects. People tend to notice things that stand out. Things tend to stand out when they change or vary against a stable background or when something stays unchanged against a changing background. For example, it is difficult for us to see birds in a forest when they are resting in trees, but when the birds fly, we notice them immediately. They are discerned from the same background when they move. As Bowden and Marton (1998) point out:

> When some aspect of a phenomenon or an event varies while another aspect or other aspects remain invariant, the varying aspect will be discerned. In order for this to happen, variation must be experienced by someone as variation. (p. 35)

In fact, even very young children can discern what is invariant in a spoken word amid the variation in tone, loudness, pitch, etc. — the meaning of the word.

The meaning we acquire of anything depends on our way of seeing it. People must be able to discern certain critical aspects of an object for them to see it in a particular way. Furthermore, we must discern all the critical aspects of a phenomenon *simultaneously* in order to gain a complete understanding of a phenomenon. Consider a detective looking at all the evidence collected from a crime scene. Some pieces of evidence are critical; others are just distracters. The detective may be looking at all the pieces of evidence that are critical for a long time without understanding what these tell him or her. When the moment comes that he or she can see these critical aspects *simultaneously*, so that their relationship to each other becomes clear, the detective will come to a new understanding of what happened, and solve the crime.

As another example, if I see or experience an object as a big, brown German shepherd dog, I should have discerned simultaneously some of its aspects, like size, colour, and breed. The meaning this object has for me is then a function of the discernment of those aspects. But how can I know that it is a big, brown German shepherd? How can I understand what a dog is if I have not encountered a dog, a cat, a cow, or other animals that I can compare it with? How can I know it is a German shepherd if I have never encountered a Terrier, a Labrador, or some other breeds of dog? And how can I tell that it is a brown dog if I have not experienced a dog of another colour? To notice or discern an aspect, we not only need to pay attention to what it is but also to what it is not. In other words, we need to experience the variation in an aspect in order to be able to discern it in one but not in another way. For example, the concepts of "size," "breed," and "colour" in the example of seeing a big, brown German shepherd are experienced as dimensions of variation with respective values such as big and small, dogs of different breeds, brown and other colours. Each dimension of variation is a critical aspect (e.g., colour), and the values (e.g., brown) are critical features.

According to Marton and Booth (1997),

> ... learning proceeds, as a rule, from an undifferentiated and poorly integrated understanding of the whole to an increased differentiation and integration of the whole and its parts ... these wholes, the learner's initial ideas, turn out to be partial rather than wrong. They are the seeds from which valid knowledge can grow. (p. viii)
>
> The whole needs to be made more distinct, and the parts need to be found and then fitted into place, like a jigsaw puzzle that sits on the table half-finished inviting the passer-by to discover more of the picture. (p. 180)

Each of the critical aspects of an object of learning contributes to the understanding of the whole, yet the aspects also bear some relationship to each other. Thus, to fully understand an object of learning, one must be able to discern how the different aspects are related to each other and how each aspect is related to the whole (Chik and Lo, 2004). Students will learn better if the teacher is able to consciously structure the teaching in such a way as to bring out the structure of the contents with clear part-part relationships and part-whole relationships, to facilitate students' discernment of these during the lesson. A more detailed account can be found in Marton and Tsui (2004).

A pedagogy based on variation

Children have to learn to be discerning, and they do not necessarily discern naturally what they need to discern. As Bransford et al. (2002) aptly point out,

> A common misconception regarding "constructivist" theories of knowing (that existing knowledge is used to build new knowledge) is that teachers should never tell students anything directly but, instead, should always allow them to construct knowledge for themselves. This perspective confuses a theory of pedagogy (teaching) with a theory of knowing ... teachers still need to pay attention to students' interpretations and provide guidance when necessary. (p. 11)

We believe that teaching should be a conscious structuring act, as the responsibility falls on the teacher in designing learning experiences that can bring about the discernment needed. Research studies undertaking this view in the past few decades (e.g., Säljö, 1975, on text comprehension; Hounsell, 1984, on essay writing; Laurillard, 1995, on problem-solving) show that, even in specified situations, qualitative differences in learning were observed. The qualities of such learning were related to the *patterns of variation* that the learners experienced with respect to the same elements of the situations, i.e., what are experienced as varying and what are not. After observing numerous lessons in the Shanghai area for many years, Gu (1991) also arrived at the same conclusion empirically, that good classroom practices are characterized by the use of appropriate patterns of variation in dealing with the objects of learning. Similar observations were made and have been recently reported in a number of studies comparing pairs of lessons with similar teaching contents in Hong Kong (Marton and Morris, 2002; Marton and Tsui, 2004). Based on the findings of these studies, Marton and Morris (2002) make the following claim about the critical conditions in classroom learning:

> The most powerful differences in how the objects of learning are dealt with are: (a) what aspects are focused on, (b) what aspects are varied simultaneously, and (c) what aspects remain invariant or constant. (p. 133)

In 2003, Marton and Runesson identified four patterns of variation that were commonly found in the lessons: *contrast, generalization, separation,* and *fusion.* Subsequently, in an advanced workshop led by Professor Ference Marton, for the research team on Learning Study at the Hong Kong Institute of Education, in November 2004, the team came to the consensus that, instead of regarding *contrast, generalization, separation,* and *fusion* as patterns of variation, it would be more appropriate to consider them possible functions that may be served by the same patterns of variation which are related to a specific object of learning. For instance, when we want to teach a child the concept "brown," we expose him or her to the experience of some other colours that are not brown (e.g., red, yellow). Here, the pattern of variation is produced by varying values of the same aspect. This enables the child to *contrast* brown with other colours and differentiate what is (i.e., example) from what is not (i.e., non-example) "brown." Then, by focusing the child's attention on what is common among different values of "colour," a dimension of variation (colour) is opened up, and colours like brown, red, and yellow are recognized as values on this dimension of variation. Thus, the same pattern of variation also serves to *separate* the abstract concept "colour" (the dimension of variation) from other aspects and hence makes possible the discernment of the concept.

However, in order for the child to fully understand the concept "brown," he or she should also experience its varying appearances ("brownness") in specific cases, such as brown chairs, brown tables, brown bookshelves, etc., to be able to *generalize* from those cases the "brownness" and distinguish it from other irrelevant aspects (e.g., "chairs," "tables," "bookshelves"). Thus, the pattern of variation, which consists of different appearances of a specific feature in a number of cases, makes it possible for the learner to make *generalizations* of the invariant principle or aspect to be discerned.

An understanding of a phenomenon or an object sometimes depends on the simultaneous awareness of several critical aspects and how these aspects relate to each other and to the phenomenon or object as a whole. The pattern of variation that involves simultaneous variation in the dimensions of variation that correspond to the critical aspects makes it possible for *fusion* to take place. For example, in order to understand what determines price, the learner must be able to experience simultaneously the variation in both the supply and demand of the same commodity, in order to be able to discern that the price of a given commodity is determined by the relative magnitude of changes in both the supply and demand of that commodity.

Therefore, different patterns of variation can be created, in different combinations and structures, to bring about different desired learning outcomes by having the learner to focus on certain aspect or aspects of the object of learning. This can be achieved by varying a certain aspect or aspects simultaneously while keeping certain aspects invariant.

Pang's (2002) study, which compared two groups of experienced teachers working together systematically on the same object of learning, revealed that the group with the specific theoretical grounding in the Theory of Variation was considerably more effective in bringing about the intended learning outcomes than the group without that explicit grounding (p. 137). If variation is the key to discernment, it should be a useful tool for structuring teaching so that the object of learning can be encountered in a particular way.

We do not advocate any particular method of teaching, and we fully acknowledge the importance of using innovative teaching methods to create learning environments that not only serve to motivate students to engage in learning but also are used as a vehicle for developing students' capabilities in the general aspect of certain objects of learning (such as being cooperative in carrying out an experiment in a group). However, we wish to point out that a gap (as represented by the dotted line in Figure 2.1), which exists in lesson preparation as practised by many teachers in Hong Kong and elsewhere, needs to be filled. There is currently too much emphasis on teaching methods, so that educational reforms are centred on innovations in teaching methods, e.g., the activity approach, project learning, problem-based learning, etc., without making reference to the content or subject matter upon which such capabilities can be built.

Lesson Preparation

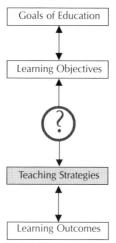

Figure 2.1 The gap that exists in lesson preparation needs to be filled

We would argue that capabilities can only be built upon specific objects of learning. Therefore, before we can start talking about what teaching methods or strategies to employ, we need first of all to ask ourselves the following questions:

- In what ways would the targeted learning outcome(s) contribute to the overall goal of education?
- What kinds of object of learning will best help us to achieve the targeted learning objective?
- How is this object of learning positioned within the overall conceptual framework for that subject matter? What kinds of pattern or relationship must be discerned in order for students to transform the factual information they have acquired into deep understanding and usable knowledge?
- What are the critical aspects of the object of learning, as reflected by students' prior understanding, knowledge, and beliefs? How can this knowledge be used as a starting point for dealing with students' learning difficulties and to help them in building new knowledge and developing deeper understanding of the object of learning?
- What kinds of pattern of variation can best be used to help students discern the critical aspects and their relationships?

Only after we have thoroughly considered the above questions would we be asking questions like the following:

- Which teaching approach would best help to achieve the intended learning outcomes?
- What methods or teaching strategies should be employed to help build a relevance structure for the students, so that all students will find what they are learning meaningful, and so are motivated and engaged?
- What methods or teaching strategies are required to facilitate the students in achieving the general aspect of a certain object of learning that is important for the learning?
- What kinds of activity would best bring out the patterns of variation to help the students learn?
- What kind of interaction in class is required, so that feedback on students' learning can be obtained during the lesson?
- What kinds of assessment can be used to provide feedback to both the students and the teachers about the effectiveness of teaching and the quality of the learning that are taking place or have taken place? Figure 2.2 summarizes the stages that we consider important in the planning of a lesson, and how the Theory of Variation helps to improve teaching and student learning outcomes.

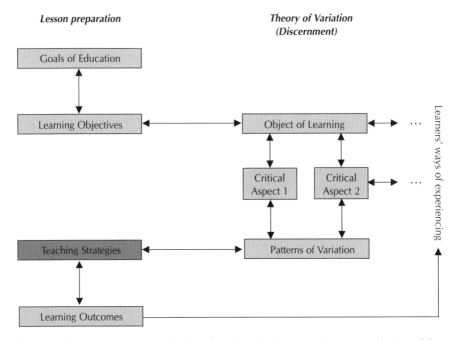

Figure 2.2 The important stages in the planning of a lesson and the contribution of the Theory of Variation to the improvement of teaching and learning

Conclusion

In the previous sections, we explained the conceptual framework we use for understanding learning, and our approach to catering for individual differences. We try to ascertain/discover the differences in the ways our students experience or think about what they are supposed to learn. From these differences, we try to identify the critical aspect(s) for the learning, thereby helping our students to learn more efficiently. In other words, we try to cater for individual differences by making use of these differences, i.e., by focusing on the students' differing perspectives as the points of departure rather than assumed difference in ability.

Knowing the critical aspects in order for planned variation to take place is not a simple task. It requires a focus on both the object of learning as well as the specific difficulties that students need to overcome in learning what is intended for them. However, our experience in teacher education tells us that good and experienced teachers are, in fact, not short of such knowledge. At the same time, it seems that such knowledge can be partial and not reflected on, let alone shared with other teachers. We try to bring about such sharing among teachers of what they know about student learning needs or difficulties by using what we consider to be a powerful tool — Learning Study. Learning Study is inspired by the Japanese Lesson Study (Stigler and Hiebert, 1999) and is a systematic process of enquiry into teaching and learning, which employs action research methodology and has the improvement of teaching and learning at its core. It takes the concerted effort of teachers, researchers, and academics working collaboratively and going through many cycles of action research for improvement, before we can get close to solving the problem of catering for individual differences. We explain our methodology in detail in Chapter 3.

We believe that learning occurs when we experience *something* in new and meaningful ways, so that the new knowledge acquired can be applied appropriately to new situations, and to illuminate new phenomena. That is to say, learning has its particular content focusing on a phenomenon or an object, and has to be related to the learners' existing ways of seeing the object concerned. To cater for individual differences, we believe that teachers should do the following:

1. Carefully select worthwhile objects of learning.
2. Identify variation in students' understanding of the intended object of learning and corresponding critical aspects that present difficulties to students' learning.
3. Plan learning experiences to help students focus on these critical aspects by making use of appropriate patterns of variation.

There are limitations to any theory, and we wish to point out that the learning Theory of Variation does not provide us with insights about the exact teaching strategies to employ. That is why we advocate that teachers and academics (researchers or teacher educators) should come together in cycles of Learning Studies, where they can contribute their expertise in content knowledge, pedagogical knowledge, as well as pedagogical content knowledge, to the planning process. A review of the literature on the teaching of that particular topic would also be very important input to ensure the quality of the resulting lesson.

3

Making Use of Learning Studies to Cater for Individual Differences

LO Mun Ling, PONG Wing Yan, and KO Po Yuk

As elaborated in Chapter 2, in order to cater for individual differences, teachers must begin from the knowledge of the different ways pupils experience and understand the object(s) of learning. This knowledge or awareness is necessary for guiding the selection of relevant learning experiences as well as for structuring the teaching task, in order to bring about the intended learning outcomes. For teachers, we will not be able to prescribe a recipe for developing such a knowledge. However, based on our experience in working with many teachers at a micro level in developing "research lessons" in a large number of "Learning Studies," we believe that teaching that is based on the above strategy can be effective in dealing with many issues related to individual differences, especially those in classroom learning.

In this chapter, we first explain the idea of "Learning Studies." We then describe a three-year project based on this idea and the results obtained. Finally, we discuss the trustworthiness of the data and its generalizability across situations.

Learning Study

The idea of "Learning Studies" originates from and is inspired by the tradition of Chinese and Japanese teachers in conducting systematic and in-depth investigations into their own lessons — the so-called "research lessons" (Lo, Marton, Pang and Pong, 2004; Lo et al., 2002; Pang and Marton, 2003). Notwithstanding that both Lesson Study and Learning Study aim to improve teaching and learning, "Learning Study" differs from "Lesson Study" as described by Stigler and Hiebert (1999) in that it is theoretically grounded (Pang and Marton, 2003). The primary focus is on an object of learning, and the Theory of Variation (Marton and Booth, 1997; Marton and Tsui, 2004; Pang, 2003) is used as a guide to achieve the object of learning, employing appropriate teaching methods. In the following, we explain our conceptual framework that builds on the idea of variation.

Building on variation

There is strong research evidence that people often hold different views about the same thing. It is therefore not difficult to imagine that students and teachers will see and experience the same subject matter differently, and the teachers may differ in seeing possible ways to handle the object of learning. Despite that, we habitually live in what the phenomenologists refer to as the "natural attitude" and take for granted that what we see and experience is exactly what the world is like, and that others see it in exactly the same way we do. To counter one's natural attitude, Bowden and Marton (1998) suggest:

> A simple and powerful way of countering the natural attitude is to make other people's ways of experiencing a certain phenomenon visible. If you do that, it becomes obvious that there are different ways of experiencing reality. … Making different ways of experiencing or understanding a certain phenomenon visible can serve aims other than countering the natural attitude. By people in a group or an organisation becoming conscious of others' ways of thinking and experiencing different phenomena, each consciousness gets linked to others and a collective consciousness arises, richer, more inclusive and, under certain circumstances, more powerful than any singular consciousness or the sum of them. (p. 41)

Therefore, our goal is to try to help students learn by enriching their ways of seeing and experiencing specific subject matters. Teachers can gain insights about students' different ways of experiencing these subject matters through listening carefully to children. Teachers' own ways of experiencing, understanding, and handling these objects of learning can be enriched by mutual sharing of their insights with colleagues, so that conscious efforts can be made in structuring relevant learning experiences for the students, guided by the Theory of Variation. In trying out ways of bringing about the learning of specific objects of learning (e.g., certain capabilities, or value to be developed, see also Chapter 2, p. 14), we are guided by three types of variation, which are elaborated in the following sections.

V1: Variation in students' understanding of the things to be taught

Students possess their own preconceptions, or intuitive understanding, of the things to be taught, even before teachers make a formal start in the classroom. These preconceptions, or beliefs about certain phenomena are often stubborn and resilient to change (see, e.g., Chinn and Brewer, 1993; Confrey, 1990; Duit and Treagust, 1998). Thus, the well-documented preconceptions or beliefs are understandably invaluable resources for designing effective instructions, because these indicate to the teacher the critical aspects that are presenting difficulties to students (Brandsford, Brown and Cocking, 2000). By paying attention to what students bring with them to the lesson, teachers are also in a better position to identify more worthwhile objects of learning, thus fostering "deep" learning in students as opposed to "shallow" learning (Marton and Säljö, 1976; Marton and Booth, 1997).

Seen from this light, students' individual differences in understanding what they are supposed to learn should be viewed as a resource for learning rather than as a constraint to learning. As there is great diversity in ability and ways of thinking among students, any group of students will produce a diverse range of ideas and solution methods that can be discussed by the whole class. And, the greater the variety of ideas generated by the group, the more benefits students will gain. In class, different students will understand the material at different levels of sophistication. If the various understandings and solution methods can be tapped, and if the class size is large enough, then the teacher is likely to obtain a whole range of responses, which will act as a vehicle for him or her to use to meet the needs of different students.

A practical question may then arise: When a teacher has to teach a class of over thirty students, how can he or she address the learning needs of each student who has a particular way of thinking? Research findings have shown that, although students are unique individuals, the *qualitatively* different ways by which they understand a particular phenomenon are always limited in number (Johansson, Marton and Svensson, 1985, on Newtonian motion; Marton, Beaty and Dall' Alba, 1993, on learning; Neuman, 1987, on number; Nussbaum, 1985, on children's conceptions of the round earth). Thus, teachers are not in a disheartening position regarding individual learning differences. What is needed is thus for teachers to be sensitized, and to nurture in themselves a capacity to understand the different ways children think about, perceive, understand, apprehend, see, and conceptualize that which they are supposed to learn, so that these differences are properly recognized, addressed, and utilized in teaching.

The different ways in which students understand the things to be taught can be found through interviewing students before the lesson, giving them a carefully set pre-test, providing them with an opportunity to express their understanding and explain their views during the lesson, and by listening carefully to what they say.

V2: Variation in teachers' ways of dealing with particular objects of learning

Teachers have daily encounters with students, and from these experiences, they are able to construct a good knowledge base about the different ways that students deal with particular concepts or phenomena, as well as a working knowledge of how to handle these differences in the lesson. This knowledge, which is referred to as "personal practical knowledge" by researchers like Elbaz (1983) and Connelly and Clandinin (1995), or "pedagogical content knowledge" by Shulman (1986), is powerful. However, it usually remains as a kind of tacit or unnoticed knowledge that teachers gain through working with children.

We view such knowledge as extremely valuable. Instead of allowing this knowledge to remain at the back of a teacher's mind, it should be identified, sharpened, and systematically reflected upon and, above all, shared with other teachers. As evident from the emerging research on teacher development, the sharing among teachers of what they know about teaching and learning can be best facilitated through collaborating in pursuing educational goals in schools and social contexts (Lieberman and Miller, 2001). Little (2001), for instance, suggests that the kind of teacher development needed for high-quality teaching and learning should be directed to learning in and from practice, and "concentrates on the combination of knowledge of subject, knowledge of teaching, and knowledge of particular groups of students" (p. 37). Cochran-Smith and Lytle (2001) also promote collaboration among teachers, specifically in inquiring about various aspects associated with their daily practice and the purposes of schooling, e.g., the daily practices of teaching and learning, and the ways different teachers and students understand them. Teachers are believed to be better able to adapt to the changing cultures of school reforms and attempt high-quality teaching and learning when a wide range of options is made possible through peer talks, analysis, and interpretations.

The variation in teachers' ways of understanding and dealing with particular objects of learning can be tapped by providing opportunities for teachers and researchers to share their ideas in preparatory meetings before the research lesson, by observing team members teach their research lessons, and by post-lesson conferences.

V3: Using variation as a guiding principle of pedagogical design

By taking into account different students' ways of knowing and understanding, the teacher is, in fact, in a better position to provide more entry points to the same object of learning. Learning from other colleagues' ways of dealing with the same content which results in different "enacted objects of learning" (Chik and Lo, 2004; Lo and Ko, 2002) can also increase teachers' understanding of the relationship between teaching and learning. Teachers should consciously make use of what has been learnt from students (V1) and from their colleagues (V2), to plan and structure their lessons.

As shown by the research studies on effective teaching and learning that focus on teaching arrangement, teacher's "academic work" (Doyle, 1983, 1986) and "planning and managing of learning tasks and activities" (Brophy, 1992) play an important role in representing the subject matter to be taught and mediating curriculum goals to be achieved in the classroom. Yet, as has been pointed out in the previous chapter, a mere focus on teaching arrangement does not guarantee deep learning. It also requires teachers to carefully consider what students are supposed to learn, and how certain arrangements work to focus students' attention on what is critical for the intended learning.

Marton's learning Theory of Variation serves as a useful theoretical framework to help teachers plan and structure their lessons. It guides teachers to decide *what aspects to focus on*, *what aspects to vary simultaneously*, and *what aspects to remain invariant or constant*; and to consciously design patterns of variation (V3) (see Chapter 2) to bring about the desired learning outcomes.

As we pointed out in Chapter 2, all theories have their limitations, and we have to be careful not to over-claim the power of a theory. The learning theory outlined above helps us to focus on the object of learning and be aware that we must first identify its critical aspects based on students' learning difficulties, so that relevant patterns of variation can be identified to increase the opportunities for students to discern these critical aspects. However, the theory does not dictate any teaching methods. We believe that there cannot be a single teaching method or approach that will be best for all objects of learning. Thus, it is very important that teachers should come together and share their wisdom. Based on their knowledge of different approaches and teaching strategies, they should discuss and come to a consensus on which strategies are best in bringing about the desired learning outcomes.

Therefore, we think that the Japanese Lesson Study model provides an excellent method for experimenting with the learning theory explained above, and would form the basis of the methodology for Learning Study. It is hoped that, by helping teachers who teach the same subject at the same level to organize themselves into small groups, better opportunities are provided for focusing on particular objects of learning. The teachers involved would work in cycles to identify and focus on the learning difficulties of students over particular objects of learning, plan and teach lessons that attempt to address those difficulties, and finally evaluate their success. As such, Learning Study, according to Marton (2001), not only serves to bring about learning in students, but in teachers as well:

> A learning study is a systematic attempt to achieve an educational objective and learn from that attempt. It is a design experiment that may or may not be a lesson study. Such a study is a learning study in two senses. First, it aims at bringing learning about, or more correctly, at making learning possible. The students will thus learn, hopefully. Second, those teachers involved try to learn from the literature, from each other, from students and not least, from the study itself. (p. 1)

Here, we wish to add that there is a third sense. In trying out the theory with Learning Study, we, as researchers, also learn from the study. Our interest would be from the perspective of teacher educators, to learn how best to help teachers to become better teachers, to help teacher educators to become better teacher educators, and to improve the methodology of Learning Study.

The three-year research project

In 2000, as was mentioned, we launched a three-year research project in which we worked with two primary schools to develop Learning Studies. Through engaging teachers in Learning Studies, we planned to sensitize teachers to their students' learning needs. In this section, we first state the objectives of the project. Then, we describe the three phases of the project, the key steps in a Learning Study cycle, and the details as regards the collection and analysis of the data.

Objectives of the project

The overall aim of the project was to investigate the extent to which Learning Study, which is premised on the three types of variation (V1, V2, and V3) as described above, could be a tool for teachers in addressing the issue of individual differences in learning in mainstream schools.

To achieve this aim, we worked with teachers from two primary schools in conducting a total of twenty-nine Learning Studies across a time span of three years. In relation to the main concern, we also attempted to answer a corollary of four sub-questions:

1. To what extent can worthwhile objects of learning, which will serve as a foundation of student learning, be identified?
2. Can the critical aspects associated with each of these objects of learning be adequately identified?
3. To what extent can a pattern or patterns of variation be identified and used in designing the lesson?
4. In what ways are the participating teachers empowered to cater for individual differences using the three types of variation?

If the answers to the above questions are positive, we should be able to see the gap between the learning outcomes of the "academic high achievers" and "academic low achievers" becoming narrower. We expect the standard deviation of the marks of the whole class to decrease, and the mean for the group with lower scores at the outset would move towards the mean of the whole class.

In the course of our investigation, we also wished to identify conditions that may enhance or limit the effect of Learning Studies in schools.

Three phases of the project

The project was to be carried out in three phases, corresponding to each year of implementation. Phase I (2000–01) was to be a year of exploration, allowing both researchers and teachers to slowly come to grips with the idea of Learning Study and the three types of variation. Phase II (2001–02) was to be a year of rapid development and consolidation, the formation of more Learning Study groups and involving more teachers. Leaders among the teachers were to be identified and trained to lead in Phase III (2002–03), during which the research team paved the way for its withdrawal from the schools. The detailed work at each of these phases is described in Chapter 4.

Main steps in a Learning Study cycle

A Learning Study group comprised teachers teaching the same subject at the same level in each school, and two or more members of the research team.[1] Each member contributed his or her own expertise, and everyone had equal status in the group. Each week, the group met for about an hour to work on a research lesson. The whole cycle took about ten to twelve weeks on average. A Learning Study went through a number of steps. These were sometimes not in a fixed sequence; some steps might occur simultaneously, and there might be iteration cycles when certain steps were revisited (see Figure 3.1). Throughout the three years of study, we modified the procedures and steps as we went through the cycles, and learnt from our mistakes and successes. Essentially, the following steps were followed:
1. Choosing and defining the object of learning, which could be capabilities or values to be developed.
2. Ascertaining students' prior understanding of the object of learning, to find out what were the possible learning difficulties (the critical aspects) before the teaching began, by pooling teachers' experiences, gathering information from research findings, giving all students a pre-lesson test, and conducting pre-lesson interviews with a sample of students. What was revealed from the student data then led to a reconsideration or redefinition of the chosen object of learning.

---

1. In some cases, the team also comprised officers of the Curriculum Development Institute (CDI).

3. Planning and implementing the research lesson(s) — with members of a group working together to establish a course of action grounded in the theory adopted. The plan was premised on an understanding of the students' existing knowledge, the teachers' experiences in handling the object of learning, as well as research studies in the related areas. After that, the teachers carried out the plan using variation to guide their lesson design in different cycles. Lesson observations and post-lesson conferences were arranged for each cycle, to facilitate the improvement of the research lesson in the next cycle, which usually involved a further refinement of the object of learning and its associated critical aspects identified in the earlier stages. All the lessons were video-recorded for analysis.

4. Evaluating the lessons — using a post-lesson test with all students and post-lesson interviews with a sample of students to find out how well the students had developed the targeted capabilities or values, and to relate the learning outcomes to the teaching act in order to improve the lesson.

5. Reporting and disseminating the results — including documenting and reporting the aims, procedures and results of the Learning Study, and disseminating the documents to other teachers and to the public. Feedback received was then used as input into the next cycle of the study.

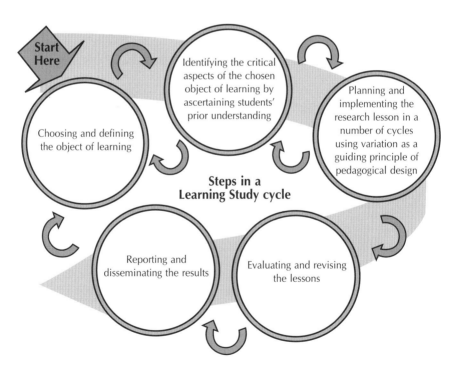

Figure 3.1 Steps in a Learning Study cycle

Changes made to refine the procedures for Learning Study over the three years of the project are summarized in Table 3.1 (as highlighted in bold and italic font).

Table 3.1 A summary of the changes made to the procedures for Learning Study over the three years of the project

2000–01	2001–02	2002–03
Stage I: Incubation of ideas		
– Choose a topic – Identify object(s) of learning and aspects that are critical for student learning		
Stage II: Lesson planning		
– Design pre-test		
	– Pilot the pre-test and/or interview a sample of students *– Revise the pre-test if needed*	
– Administer and analyse data collected from the finalized pre-test – Plan for the lesson		
Stage III: Lesson implementation		
– Implement the lesson with all classes	*– Implement the lesson by one of the teachers in the group (first cycle)* *– Debriefing on the first cycle of lesson conducted, and revise the lesson plan if needed* *– Implement the lesson with the remaining classes*	*– Implement the lesson by the teachers in the group in a number of cycles* *– Debriefing on each cycle of lesson conducted, and/or interview a sample of students after each cycle* *– Revise the lesson plan if needed*
– Videotape each lesson conducted		
Stage IV: Evaluation		
– Administer and analyse data collected from the post-test – Reflect on student performances in both the pre-test and post-test, and in class – Evaluate the actual enactments of the lessons and their effectiveness		
Stage V: Reporting and Dissemination		
	Report and disseminate their research experiences within the school and to the public	

Data collection

In this project, the main sources of data came from the Learning Studies and the teacher interviews.

Learning Studies

A total of twenty-nine learning studies were developed for different topics in the four subject areas of Chinese language, mathematics, general studies, and English language during the past three academic years (2000/2001, 2001/ 2002, 2002/2003). Table 3.2 summarizes the details of the Learning Study groups and the number of research lessons carried out in the three years of the project.

The data collected for the Learning Studies include audio recordings and notes of regular meetings, lesson plans, video recordings of the research lessons, pre- and post-test papers completed by the students, and/or recordings of student interviews.

Table 3.2 Summary of the Learning Studies carried out in the three years of the project

Year / School	2000–01	2001–02	2002–03
	Learning study group (number of research lessons conducted)		
School 1	P4 Chinese language (3)	P4 Chinese language (2) P5 Chinese language (2) P3 General studies (2)	P6 Chinese language (1) P4 General studies (1) P4 English language (1)
School 2	P1 Mathematics (2) P4 Mathematics (2)	P1 Mathematics (2) P2 Mathematics (2) P4 Mathematics (2) P5 Mathematics (2) P4 Chinese language (2)	P3 Mathematics (1) P4 General studies (1) P6 Mathematics (1)

Teacher interviews

Individual interviews with thirty-seven and thirty-one participant teachers were carried out in the academic years 2001/2002 and 2002/2003 respectively, to explore their views about the project. All the interviews were audio-recorded and transcribed subsequently, for further analysis.

Additional data sources

Additional sources of data came from the written comments of some of the participating teachers, the school principals, and the representative of the Curriculum Development Institute (the funding body) who took part in some of the Learning Studies. The data from the Hong Kong Attainment Test of the group of students who were involved in all three years of the project were followed longitudinally and studied for triangulation purposes.

Data analysis

A case study was built from the data collected for each Learning Study. All sources of data collected from the twenty-nine Learning Studies were carefully studied to draw insights and to address our research concerns. In particular, the conceptual framework of variation described above was employed for the data analysis, focusing on the following aspects:

- The worthiness of the object of learning and the corresponding critical aspects identified for each research lesson.
- The pattern(s) of variation created in each Learning Study, and the effect on students of different academic performance.
- Student learning. Students' learning outcomes are mainly based on the analysis of the videotaped research lesson, and pre- and post-test results. The same test was administered to the students before and after the research lesson. The pre-test results provided baseline data, so that the difference between the pre- and post-test results gave an indication of how well students had learnt. Students who scored equal to or less than the first quartile and those who scored equal to or more than the third quartile on the pre-test were regarded as "weaker" and "stronger" respectively in understanding the chosen topic, and their performance was traced. In some cases, interviews of a selected number of students (perceived by the teacher to be of high, medium, or low ability) were also conducted to probe students' understanding of the object of learning.
- The relationship between teaching and learning. One major use of the pre- and post-test results was to illuminate the relationship between students' different learning outcomes and the teachers' different ways of dealing with the object of learning. As each research lesson went through several cycles of evaluation, re-planning and re-teaching, there were bound to be modifications to the research lesson. In addition, the teachers necessarily taught differently in response to varying dynamic classroom situations. These differences, which were captured on video, provided us with the opportunity for identifying the relationship between how well students learnt and how teachers actually taught. This knowledge is vital in improving teaching and learning in schools.
- The impact of Learning Study on teachers' professional development. The teachers were interviewed after the first cycle of Learning Study in the second and third years of the project. The interviews were audio-recorded and transcribed. They were then analysed to find out whether the teachers understood the Theory of Variation and were able to apply it in their subject, had benefited from working collaboratively, had greater awareness of students' prior experiences and the possible difficulties they might encounter in any object of learning, and were more confident in handling individual differences in class.

- Factors that facilitated and hindered the implementation of the Learning Studies in the two schools.

Trustworthiness of data

For the authors, Learning Study is an on-going project. At the time of writing, a large number of Learning Studies have been and are being undertaken, which we believe will provide data to further verify our claims. However, we argue that it would be more appropriate to view our methodology as one belonging to the qualitative research tradition rather than to quantitative experimentation research. In this regard, we find the concept of "trustworthiness" (Lincoln and Guba, 1985), a criterion most used in judging naturalistic studies, most pertinent (instead of using the traditional concepts of validity and reliability). Bassey (1999, 75) delineates the concept of trustworthiness into eight questions, which we answer in turn below:

1. *Has there been prolonged engagement with data sources?*
   For the Learning Studies we conducted, we spent an average of about three months on each one in working with the teachers involved. However, the data generated and collected over the three months for each Learning Study were analysed and studied well beyond that period. The engagement with the data did not stop after the Learning Studies were finished. We continued to analyse the data and tried to interpret what each research lesson was telling us about students' learning and the relationship to teaching. Many of the Learning Studies were presented to the public and then reinterpreted, based on the comments obtained from the audience, peers, and other teachers. Using the knowledge gained from our experience (e.g., new patterns of variations), some of the data were re-analysed. Throughout the three years of the project, each new Learning Study brought new understanding to the previous studies.

2. *Has there been persistent observation of emerging issues?*
   The team was sensitive to emerging issues and had taken measures to deal with them. This was reflected in the way the procedure for conducting Learning Study was modified over the three-year period.

3. *Have raw data been adequately checked with the sources?*
   The raw data collected for the Learning Studies were authentic materials, including the audio recordings and notes of regular meetings, the video recordings of the research lessons, the pre- and post-test papers completed by students, and recordings of student interviews. All interview recordings were transcribed subsequently, for further analysis.

4. *Has there been sufficient triangulation of raw data leading to analytical statements?*
    The different data sources were triangulated before assertion was made. For instance, evidence of students' learning was obtained from the pre- and post-tests, student interviews, teachers' perception, as well as lesson observations. Indications of teachers' professional development were found from interviews, and triangulated with their contributions in research meetings and their actual teaching, as well as their performance in dissemination seminars.

5. *Has the working hypothesis, evaluation, or emerging story been systematically tested against the analytical statements?*
    Each Learning Study was carefully analysed to see whether the pattern(s) of variation created was effective in helping the students of different abilities to grasp the critical aspect(s) identified for their learning of a particular object of learning. Data from all twenty-nine Learning Studies were also cross-examined, to draw insights to improve the process.

6. *Has a critical friend thoroughly tried to challenge the findings?*
    An external consultant from the funding agency provided feedback annually during the three-year period. Some of the Learning Studies of the two project schools were presented in seminars for public scrutiny. Each of these seminars had audiences of over 100 teachers.

7. *Is the account of the research sufficiently detailed to give the reader confidence in the findings?*
    Two half-yearly progress reports and two annual reports have been produced and were submitted by the research team to the Curriculum Development Institute. Detailed reports of selected Learning Studies are appended in these reports, as well as in the final report, to include enough details to show the readers how the assertions were arrived at. For teachers' interviews, we quoted the informant's own words to reveal the perceptions.

8. *Does the case record provide an adequate audit trail?*
    All videotapes, meeting notes, test papers, and interview transcriptions have been kept and are available.

Generalizability

The work that we have conducted in Learning Study can be described as a series of case studies, each contributing to one another as time goes by. However, the researchers are still faced with the usual question of generalizability that is asked of research of this nature. We understand that there are diverse views within educational research on whether it is appropriate to expect a high level of generalizability of case study research. While authors such as Cohen and Manion (1994) argue that the purpose of studying an individual case is to probe deeply and to analyse intensively the multifarious phenomena that constitute the life cycle of the case with a view to establishing generalization about the wider population to which that unit belongs (pp. 106–7), others researchers such as Yin (1993, 50) point out that a case study does not represent a sample, and its purpose is to form theoretical propositions and not to generalize to populations or universes. We believe that both arguments have merits. However, we wish to point out that our aim and preference is on drawing theoretical conclusions regarding the value of Learning Studies in improving teaching and learning and in addressing the issue of individual differences.

In our project, we worked with two project schools and carried out a total of twenty-nine Learning Studies over a period of thirty-six months. The project has created a great amount of data. Knowing that teaching and learning in the classroom is a dynamic process which is subject to the influence of numerous varying contextual factors (e.g., school setting, students' needs), we are reluctant to predict if teachers who have not participated in any of our Learning Studies will be able to replicate our results by repeating what our teachers have done with their students. Rather, we believe that other teachers, in Hong Kong or elsewhere, by learning about Learning Studies via various means (e.g., through reading this book, reading the Learning Study reports, learning about it through public seminars or our website), will be able to gain insights from the theoretical propositions of the project. They should be able to set up their own Learning Studies in a similar way, produce effects on their students' learning, and eventually improve their own teaching practice.

4

Learning Studies: Development and Impact

LO Mun Ling, Pakey CHIK Pui Man, KO Po Yuk, Allen LEUNG Yuk Lun, PONG Wing Yan, Priscilla LO-FU Yin Wah, and Dorothy NG Fung Ping

In this chapter, we begin with an overall description of the development of the project over the three academic years. This is then followed by a close examination of what we have achieved, according to the criteria we suggested in Chapter 2. The impact of the project on the development of the two project schools and the project's dissemination activities within the teaching community is also described.

The three-year development of the project

The development of the project consisted of three phases, each taking one academic year to accomplish its goals.

Phase I: Exploration and preparation

Phase I was a year of exploration and preparation. In this phase, we primarily aimed at setting up an infrastructure within the two project schools, to facilitate the research team's collaboration. This included setting up a website for the maintenance of an on-line database of Learning Studies accessible to all participants. A total of eight research lessons were carried out by four groups of teachers teaching Chinese language (Primary 4) and mathematics (Primary 1 and 4) in the two schools. We also aimed at familiarizing the teachers with the rationale and the theoretical framework of the project, by means of seminars and workshops. In this phase, both researchers and teachers were slowly coming to grips with the ideas of Learning Study and Variation in practice. Although there were many previous studies in mathematics that contributed to the understanding of students' learning in various mathematics topics and so greatly helped the design of the research lessons, such knowledge was not available for the research lessons on Chinese language. Even so, we were very happy to find that, in all the groups engaging in Learning Studies in both schools, the teachers were discovering diverse ways of making use of variation in their lesson design. Such an approach to theory building and development, which is grounded in practice, contributes greatly to the advancement of the Theory of Variation as applied to the two subjects: Chinese language and mathematics.

Phase II: Development and consolidation

The second year was a year of development and consolidation. We aimed to enhance the capability of the teacher participants in implementing the approach adopted in the project, and to build on what had been established in the two schools in Phase I. More Learning Study groups were organized to involve more teachers. After one year of experience, both researchers and teachers became familiar with the use of the theoretical framework to locate students' difficulties or problems and to use variation to plan the research lessons. The methodology of Learning Study also became more complete by adding in some new elements to ensure the effective collection of student data (e.g., carrying out post-lesson student interviews) and modification of the lesson plans (e.g., holding post-lesson conferences immediately after lesson observations). The resulting research lessons were of higher quality. In this phase, a total of sixteen research lessons were conducted by eight groups of teachers teaching Chinese language (two Primary 4 and one Primary 5), mathematics (Primary 1, 2, 4 and 5) and general studies (Primary 3). We also invited the participant teachers to disseminate their experiences to other teachers in their own schools as well as in public seminars open to all teachers in Hong Kong.

Phase III: Capacity building and preparation for withdrawal

In Phase III, we began to pave the way for our withdrawal from the schools and focused our efforts on the capacity building of the leaders so that the practice of Learning Studies could take root in the schools. To ensure that teachers had a deep understanding of the theoretical underpinnings and how Learning Study works in the four subjects of Chinese language, English language, mathematics, and general studies, we carried out fewer Learning Studies but spent more time with the groups. The methodology of Learning Study was further fine-tuned to enhance more systematic and smooth running of the studies. Six research lessons (one P6 Chinese language, one P4 English language, one P3 and one P6 mathematics, and two P4 general studies) were produced by six groups of teachers. A number of teachers emerged as leaders while taking up more responsibilities in the Learning Studies groups. These teachers were expected to continue to take the lead in running Learning Study cycles in their schools after the research team withdrew at the end of the project. More emphasis and opportunities were also provided for the teachers to report and disseminate their research lessons and to share their experiences.

Impact of the project

Improving the curriculum

As we have explained, the identification of objects of learning and their corresponding critical aspects contributes significantly to our knowledge about the design of curriculum and how it can be strengthened for addressing individual differences in learning. In this section, we give some examples to illustrate the contributions of the Learning Studies in this area.

Identifying worthwhile objects of learning

To maximize the learning of all students in the class, and to make sure that all can progress in their study, we have to make sure that there will not be any essential knowledge missed or left partially understood. Most teachers in Hong Kong are very dependent on their textbooks. However, for any given text in a textbook, there are many different interpretations of what is worthwhile. Some objects of learning are more worthwhile than others, because they bring about more powerful ways of seeing. The following are two examples that illustrate this point.

Example 1: Primary 4 Chinese language, "A short pencil"

In teaching Chinese text comprehension, the teachers were used to a traditional set of teaching procedures focusing only on the understanding of a text, acquisition of some new vocabulary, and the learning of some sentence patterns. In this Learning Study, the teachers had to deal with a text that told the story of a boy who threw away a short pencil three times. However, instead of following the traditional set of teaching procedures, they would look for something that was worth learning in the text. After close examination of the text, they found that the same action (throwing away the short pencil) appeared three times in the text, yet the sentiment of the boy conveyed in each case was different. The teachers decided that it would be worthwhile to draw attention to how the choice of verbs matched the actions and the verbal expressions to show escalating feelings of dislike. Thus, the object of learning became: *the ability to discern that the verb used to show a certain action, the verbal expressions, and the feelings of the actor must all match.*

Also, in the text, there are five words ("receive" [接], "fish out" [掏], "carry" [提], "pick up" [撿], "throw" [抛]) with the "hand radical" [扌]). They are all synonyms of the word [拿] (meaning "take") and are associated with some actions using the hand. Yet, each word has a slightly different meaning. The teachers decided that another worthwhile object of learning would be: *the ability to distinguish the subtle difference in meaning and usage of each of these words.* This would help students in writing since the use of words has to be more precise to convey the exact meaning in the written language.

Thus, in this case, the objects of learning identified are more worthwhile goals to achieve than the traditional ones, as they expand students' language ability and help to build a firm foundation for writing.

Example 2: Primary 4 English language, "Subject-verb agreement in simple present tense"

When planning for their first Learning Study in English language, a group of Primary 4 teachers was faced with a text in their textbook that explained the different professions and what these people do. The focus of the lesson could be placed on the different professions, and the vocabulary concerning what they do, e.g., doctor — treats sick people, cook — cooks meals, driver — drives cars, etc. However, the teachers were also concerned about their students' inability to conform to subject-verb agreement in simple present tense. Thus, instead of following the routine suggested in the textbook, which focused on teaching sentence patterns and vocabulary, the teachers decided to deal with the problem of subject-verb agreement in the research lesson.

Thus, on the topic of "talking about professions" in their textbook, the object of learning was redefined as: *the capability to conform to subject-verb agreement in the simple present tense in talking about professions using the "what is/are" and "what do/does" patterns.* In this way, the learning became more powerful, as it helped to build a foundation for learning about subject-verb agreement in the simple present tense.

Discussions among the teachers provide an opportunity to identify which objects of learning are most worthwhile, as illustrated in the above examples. Experiences from previous studies also contribute to teachers' decisions about the more worthwhile objects of learning. However, as the Learning Study proceeds, there is still flexibility to redefine the objects of learning, based on, for example, results from the pre-test and/or the student interviews. The following is an example:

Example 3: Primary 1 mathematics, "Contextualized problems of addition and subtraction"

Following a successful attempt in the previous year, the Learning Study group intended to continue to focus their study on contextualized problems of simple addition and subtraction. Initially, they wanted students to be able to distinguish conceptually the meaning of addition and subtraction, which seemed to be difficult for the previous year's students. However, surprisingly, the students did extremely well on the pre-test. Almost 90 percent of them obtained a perfect score on all five questions, some individual classes producing even better results. Obviously, the results did not confirm the teachers' expectations, which were based on their experience with their previous year's students. The students were now different. The pre-test results led the team to re-think the "object of learning." There was no point in teaching what the students already knew, because they would not be challenging them at the edge of their current competence. So, there was a need to modify the "object of learning" and aim higher for the purpose of the research lesson. The teachers thus went back to the research literature in mathematics teaching to find out what would constitute a worthwhile objective in the students' progression of learning contextualized problems at this level.

The teachers decided that there was a need to be more specific about the kinds of addition and subtraction problem to be taught. The choices for these were: canonical versus non-canonical problems, the "change," "combine," "compare," or "equalize" types of problem. The final decision was to focus on non-canonical problems of a "change" nature (e.g., "There is a box of cake. Siu Ming has eaten three pieces of the cake, and there are five pieces left in the box. How many pieces of cake were there in the box at the beginning?") and "combine" nature (e.g., "Siu Fun needs eight balloons. She has already got three. How many more balloons does she need?"). These indeed proved to be most difficult for the students on a second pre-test. Thus, in this case, the learning was pitched at the right level of difficulty and the object of learning was chosen to maximize student learning.

Identifying learning gaps

Students often brought with them various misconceptions or misinterpretations that were found to be associated with their intuitive or prior understanding about the chosen subject matter. However, these were sometimes omitted or overlooked in the curriculum, thus leaving gaps to be filled before students could learn and understand the new subject matter. The consideration of whether an object of learning is worthwhile can be based on how well it helps to fill these gaps. In the following examples, learning gaps were identified and dealt with.

Example 1: Primary 2 mathematics, "Quadrilaterals: features of rectangles and parallelograms"

The topic of study was "quadrilaterals." Reference was made to the textbook which defined six types of quadrilateral, each with particular features such as "opposite sides are equal," "opposite angles are equal," "four sides are equal," etc. However, it was found from the pre-test results that many students had difficulty grasping the concept of the "opposite angle" of an angle in a given quadrilateral. To these young students, all the three other angles in the quadrilateral "looked" opposite to the one given. This way of "seeing" angles in a quadrilateral would give these students a disadvantage in discerning different properties of quadrilaterals, e.g., how to distinguish between a parallelogram and a rectangle, or between a square and a rhombus. Thus, instead of teaching the features of the six types of quadrilateral as described in the textbook, the teachers decided to focus on the features of rectangles and parallelograms first and in particular, to clarify students' various conceptions of "opposite angles."

Subsequently, the content of the lesson was made more focused, and changed from "the features of the six types of quadrilateral" to "the features of rectangles and parallelograms." One of the critical aspects that required special attention was the ability to discern the "opposite angle" of any given angle in a rectangle or parallelogram. Thus, this lesson became a very important "scaffolding" activity. A mastery of this concept was considered to be able to help students identify pairs of opposite angles in other quadrilaterals — square and rhombus — at a later stage.

Example 2: Primary 4 general studies, "The colour of light"

Being able to identify the seven colours of a rainbow as red, orange, yellow, green, blue, indigo, and violet was one of the learning objectives stated in the school's Primary 3 general studies textbook. The composition of the seven colours into white light (sunlight) was another. However, the teachers found from the pre-test that, although most students could readily recite the seven colours of a rainbow, they did not have the concept that white light is composed of different colours and so can be split up to show a rainbow which, in turn, can be "recombined" to form white light.

It was therefore decided that, for the research lesson, a more worthwhile object of learning would be: *conceptual understanding of the relationship between white light (or sunlight) and the spectrum of a rainbow.* That would mean knowing that white light is composed of lights of different colours (in fact, a spectrum of colours and not just seven), and that it is possible for white light to be split up into its component colour lights. Then, of course, these colour lights can be recombined (focused) to form white light.

To identify the critical aspects, we interviewed some students to discover their possible misconceptions and preconceptions. A major misconception revealed was that the students tended to associate the appearance of the rainbow with the prism rather than with sunlight. Some students thought that, when sunlight struck the prism, the prism gave off a rainbow.

Therefore, in dealing with the object of learning, two aspects were identified as critical: the prism is only a tool used to split up the white light, and there is a direct relationship between white light and the spectrum of a rainbow.

Building a professional knowledge base which informs curriculum development

The data of students' different understanding of the chosen objects of learning collected by various means (including the pre-tests, post-tests, student interviews, and lesson observations) were also valuable resources for curriculum development. Across the three years of study, some of the Learning Studies were repeated in different cycles by different groups of teachers, either in the same school in different years or in different schools within a year. As more information about students' various misconceptions or misinterpretations in learning the chosen topics surfaced through having a larger population and greater variety of students, the objects of learning and the associated critical aspects/features were being continuously refined. All these then contributed to form a more coherent and meaningful curriculum.

Example 1: Primary 3 general studies, "The properties of water"

The initial plan for this research lesson was to deal with the concepts of "water and solution," "the three states of water and the water cycle," and "boiling and evaporation." However, after the first cycle of the Learning Study, we found from the results of the post-test that some of the students still had difficulty grasping the concept of "the water cycle," and in particular the concepts of "evaporation" and "condensation." As revealed during a post-lesson interview with some students, the problem lay in the fact that the students were not convinced that there is water vapour in air. The beliefs that "the water droplets on the surface of a cold drink are brought out from the refrigerator or caused by the water inside the can leaking out" were still persistent. Some students also thought that the water vapour emerging from the boiling water would finally disappear in air, and some even thought that the water vapour turned into air, e.g., oxygen. Thus, the teachers found that there were two other critical features that needed to be attended to:

- *There is water vapour in air, which is invisible.*
- *Water vapour in the air condenses when it meets a cold surface.*

A second cycle of the Learning Study was developed to deal with these newly found critical aspects. For example, to confront the misconception that the water droplets on a cold drink came from the liquid in the can, the teacher poured out the cold drink and showed that water droplets were still formed on the surface of the can. To show that there was water vapour in air, the students investigated what happened when the cold can was placed in different parts of the classroom. They found that water droplets were formed whenever there was air.

In the third cycle, three terms in Chinese were further introduced to represent steam （蒸氣）, water vapour （水蒸氣）, which is visible, and water vapour in air （水汽）, which is invisible. We also decided to add in one more variation to help students see that since the water droplets came from water vapour in air, if there was no air, then there should not be any water formed on the surface of the cold drink. The teacher first dried the surface of a cold drink and then wrapped it with dry tissue paper. Then the teacher quickly wrapped a layer of Glad Wrap™ over this. Outside, she wrapped it with another layer of tissue paper. It was found that the outer layer of tissue paper (which was in contact with air) became wet while the inside layer (which was not in contact with air) remained dry. The students were able to draw the conclusion from their observations that the water condensing on the surface of the can came from air. This research lesson was also carried out in another school.

Each cycle of the study helped us to deal with the topic better, so that students with the identified misconceptions would not encounter learning difficulties. However, we had not yet exhausted all possible misconceptions. For example, there were some students who thought that water vapour turned into air (not as a component in a mixture, but as oxygen, hydrogen, etc.) This misconception still has to be dealt with in subsequent research lessons. But, as teachers are teaching more effectively, the percentage of students with difficulties will decrease, and teachers can then spend more time listening to these students, finding out what is hindering them from understanding, and then plan their teaching accordingly. A fourth cycle of this study had, in fact, been completed in another school, under another project: the Progressive and Innovative Primary Schools Project supported by the "Quality Education Fund."

Thus, in this case, the Learning Study was repeated in different cycles that took place in different schools. This resulted in more information about students' various misconceptions of the topic being drawn from a wider setting. The more we can find out about possible misconceptions, the better the position we are in to help students learn effectively, thus catering for their differences in learning, which may be brought about by ambiguity in the textbook and gaps in the curriculum. The knowledge acquired of what is critical for helping students to develop deep understanding in the object of learning could also be transferred and further developed in schools.

Example 2: Appreciation and the use of simile in modern Chinese poetry

The school developed three Learning Studies in Chinese language that built on each other with the same group of students across the three years of study.

The first Learning Study was on modern Chinese poetry (Primary 4), the objects of learning being:

- The rules governing the syllabic of modern Chinese poetry (syllable arrangement, rhyming, and the use of concise language).
- The capability in writing modern Chinese poetry that follows the set of rules.

The second Learning Study was on "simile" with the same group of students (Primary 5). The objects of learning were as follows:

- The format and the function of simile.
- The capability to appreciate and use simile in writing.

In the third year, these teachers decided to build on what the students had learnt in the previous two years, so that their knowledge of both writing modern poetry and simile were put together, reinforced, and advanced. The object of learning identified for this Learning Study was:

- The capability to appreciate and use appropriate and novel similes in writing modern Chinese poetry.

In this case, the teachers, inspired by the first two Learning Studies, developed another study, further deepening the students' understanding of the subject matters. This illustrates how a professional knowledge base of teaching could be established and used to inform school-based curriculum development that took into account how students of different interests and needs progress in learning.

A total of 29 Learning Studies were carried out to develop research lessons in the subjects of mathematics (14), Chinese language (10), general studies (4), and English language (1) throughout the three years of study. Each Learning Study focused on a particular object of learning and the corresponding critical aspects/features. (A summary of the objects of learning and the corresponding critical aspects/features identified for each Learning Study is provided in Appendix 1.)

In all the Learning Studies we have done so far, all the objects of learning belong to the cognitive domain; none of the Learning Studies tackled other domains such as skills, attitudes, or values. This was for two reasons:

a. We respect the teachers' choice. Teachers tended to be cautious when they first tried out the Learning Study, and preferred to tackle an object of learning that they perceived to be easier.
b. Teachers are more concerned with improving the learning of certain topics in the curriculum than they are with the development of attitudes and values.

At a later stage, in our other research projects, Learning Studies on both skills and values were developed. For example, one Learning Study on the topic of resources on Earth included "an awareness of conservation" as one of the objects of learning for a group of Primary 5 students. In another study, the "skills of observation" was the focus of a Learning Study for a group of Primary 1 students.

Developing variation as a guiding principle of pedagogical design: Structuring lessons by patterns of variation

In each Learning Study, conscious effort was made to structure the research lesson to make it possible for students to discern the critical aspects/features associated with the identified object of learning through particular patterns of variation — certain aspects of the identified object of learning were kept invariant while others varied. The post-test was then used as a major means to show the progress that the students had made with regard to the intended learning outcomes. In some of the studies, lesson observations and post-lesson conferences were arranged between different cycles of the research lessons, and adjustments were made to improve on the patterns of variation.

As noted in Chapter 2, a particular pattern of variation can serve different functions (contrast, generalization, separation, and fusion), depending on what is to be focused upon in the lesson. The following are some examples illustrating how lessons were structured in practice, and how a particular pattern of variation functions to enhance students' learning of specific objects of learning in different subject areas.

Example 1: P4 general studies, "The colour of light"

One misconception that many students had about the prism is that it would give out a rainbow when struck by sunlight. To help students discern that the prism is only a tool, which is an abstract concept, students must experience variation in the tools used to split up white light into a rainbow. Therefore, in the research lesson, both white light and the rainbow were kept invariant while the tool used to split up the white light was varied, e.g., using a prism, soap bubbles, and small water droplets. By drawing the students' attention to the varying tools while keeping the other components invariant, a dimension of variation in the tool aspect was separated off, which served to facilitate the discernment that prisms and other tools (i.e., the values on the dimension of variation) are only tools used to split white light into a spectrum. This is an example of "separation."

Example 2: Primary 2 mathematics, "Prisms and cylinders"

In this research lesson, students were expected to be able to discern the defining features of prisms and cylinders (the object of learning). Groups of students tried to construct models of two given objects (a triangular prism and a rectangular prism) using plastic sticks and connectors. Next, groups of students were given a tool kit to construct a cylinder. The students then compared their constructions of prisms and cylinders, and generalized from these examples (varying appearances of prism) common features of prisms and cylinders (the invariant aspects). This is an example of "generalization" since the students were required to focus on and discern what is invariant across different examples of prism. The following are the conclusions reached by the students during their discussion:

- There are two "tops" (or "upper surface and lower surface") on each prism. These two "tops" are identical in shape and size.
- Prisms have "thickness."
- The side edges of a prism are straight, equal in length, and parallel to each other.
- A cylinder is a special case in which the two "tops" are circles and there are no side edges.

To conclude, students were presented with a number of three-dimensional objects, including prisms of different sizes and shapes, cylinders of different sizes, and other objects like cones. They were then asked to categorize these objects using the features they had arrived at in the previous activities. Two categories resulted: prisms and cylinders, and non-prisms (e.g., cones). In order to be able to categorize these objects, students had to be aware at the same time that some of the objects shared the same features of prisms and cylinders listed above, and are thus prisms and cylinders, despite the fact that they are different in values in each of those aspects. For example, the objects classified as prisms have thickness, yet some of them are thinner (e.g., a coin) than the others (e.g., a chocolate box). This is an example of "fusion."

Using a diagnostic test that assessed the students' understanding of the concepts of prisms, the performance of 182 Primary 2 students before and after the research lesson was compared. On the pre-test, *4.5% of students* could write down some general properties of prisms. On the post-test, *56% of students* could correctly explain why the specific object was not a prism by using the properties of prisms discussed in class. This is especially encouraging because, according to their teachers, Primary 2 students usually cannot explain themselves clearly in written language.

A score of eight is full marks, but only 2% of students scored six or seven, and no one scored eight on the pre-test. On the post-test, 25% of students scored above six. The number of students who scored zero or one dropped tremendously from 47% (pre-test) to 7% (post-test). The performance of ten academically weaker students (two from each class) was also traced for comparison. These students scored two or below in the pre-test but had improved greatly up to an average of 6.7 out of eight on the post-test, a gain score of 5.2. This was encouraging when compared to the average gain score of the whole Primary 2 level of 2.5, from 1.8 (pre-test) up to 4.3 (post-test).

Example 3: Primary 6 Chinese language , "Appreciation and the use of simile in writing modern Chinese poetry"

The object of learning of this lesson was identified as students' capability in using an appropriate simile in writing modern poems. One of the critical features is the appropriateness of the use of a simile: the three major components of a simile (subject [本體], post-modifier [喻體], and connotation [喻解]) should match one another. To enable students to be aware of this feature, a pattern of variation was employed in the research lesson, based upon the following rhyme (the lyrics of a song "小幼苗" by Cheng Kwok Kwong): *A baby in the sun is like a seedling — can't leave you swaying in wind and rain.* [陽光中的寶寶如幼苗，難讓你在風裏搖，雨中飄]

First, the teacher replaced the word "seedling" with "weed" and asked the students to explain why the revised simile was inappropriate. Here, variation was introduced in the post-modifier while the other parts of the simile were kept invariant to allow the students to see by contrasting the two versions of the simile that the former did not match the latter. Then, the teacher replaced the word "in the sun" by "in a war" and the students again had to explain why this was inappropriate. This time, the subject varied and the other parts were kept invariant, to allow the students to see the mismatch between the subject and the rest of the revised simile. Next, the students were asked to suggest post-modifiers other than "seedling," which can be matched with the given subject ("a baby in the sun") and connotation ("can't leave you swaying in wind and rain") to form an appropriate simile. A dimension of variation in the post-modifiers with other parts of the simile remained invariant was thus opened up and served the function of "generalization" since the students were required to focus on the invariant feature of an appropriate simile, i.e., the different components of a simile should match one another.

The next example shows how variation was used to enable the students to discern by contrasting two ways of structuring the poem that the connotation of a simile has to match the subject and the post-modifier. This was achieved by mixing up the different stanzas of a poem that consists of different similes describing the movements of a small boat:[1]

---

1. This poem was written by a student Lam Ngar Li (林雅莉) and published in Mandarin Daily News on 19 July 1997.

The small boat is like the cradle of my babyhood [小船像我幼時的搖籃]
Gently, tenderly [輕輕柔柔的]
Swaying in a river [在河上搖晃]
……
The small boat is like a swing that I like to play on [小船像我愛玩的盪鞦韆]
In an endless flow of water [在無盡的流域裏]
Rocking higher and higher [愈盪愈高]

The teacher made up a new stanza by replacing the first sentence of the second stanza with the first sentence of the first stanza. The teacher then asked the students to decide whether it was appropriate or not.

The small boat is like the cradle of my babyhood [小船像我幼時的搖籃上]
In an endless flow of water [在無盡的流域裏]
Rocking higher and higher [愈盪愈高]

Here, an inappropriate simile was made up to allow the students to contrast it with the original one, to see the critical feature of a simile.

The following is an excerpt of a post-lesson interview with a group of students, in the last cycle of the research lesson. During the interview, the researcher invited the students to comment on the simile used in one of the poems created in class. The students were able to make use of what they had learnt in the lesson to assess and even to revise the simile so that it became more appropriate.

Researcher (*reading aloud a poem created in class*): "The ocean is like mother and daughter. In the time of flood tide, it is like a mother covering her daughter with a blanket. In the time of ebb tide, it is like the daughter kicking off the blanket." What do you think about this poem?

Student 1: It will be more appropriate if it can be changed to "Ocean and beach," because the ocean is... like a blanket. But it cannot show the relationship between mother and daughter. ... The subject and the post-modifier used in the poem are not appropriate.

Researcher: What should be changed?

Student 2: The subject.

Researcher: ... what should it be changed into?

Student 1: Ocean ... and beach.

Researcher: What about the sentences?

Student 1: "Ocean and beach are like mother and daughter." ... We can keep the rest of the sentences using the same connotation.

Example 4: Primary 4 English language, "Subject-verb agreement in simple present tense"

In the research lesson, students were expected to show increased ability in conforming to subject-verb agreement in talking about professions in the simple present tense (the object of learning). To achieve this, it is important for students to be aware of the relationship between the subject item (one of the critical aspects) and the verb form (another critical aspect) in a given sentence, i.e., when the subject item is the third person singular ("he" or "she"), "s/es" should be added to the verb.

The lesson began with revision of the three professions taught in the previous lesson. Then, students were asked to describe the nature of the professions one by one. For each profession, the teacher asked a "what" question three times, varying the subject item among "he," "she," and "they" by showing corresponding pictures (i.e., "What does he/she do?" and "What do they do?"). In response, students were to choose between singular and plural verb forms to answer the questions (i.e., "He/She *drives* buses." and "They *drive* buses.") Thus, each time students were to decide on the verb form, they had to be aware of the variation in the subject item. In other words, they had to experience the subject item and the verb form at the same time (an example of "fusion"). This pattern of questions was repeated for the three professions, and students were helped to arrive at the relationship between the subject item and the verb form in a given sentence, which was then summarized in a table. To consolidate, students formed groups to play a matching game and then to work on a worksheet. In these activities, students were again required to decide on the appropriate answer with proper matching between the subject item and the verb form. This is an example of "fusion" since the subject item and the verb form varied at the same time, to facilitate the students' discernment of the subject-verb agreement. After students completed the worksheet, teachers went over the work with the class. Correct answers were contrasted with incorrect answers (an example of "contrast").

The performance of 73 Primary 4 students who attended both the pre-test and post-test was compared. On average, 14% more of the students (from 37% on the pre-test to 52% on the post-test) were found to be able to use the appropriate verb form corresponding to the subject item in a sentence pattern similar to the one used in the lesson (e.g., "What does Mary do every day? *She brushes* her teeth every day."). Since it was the practice of the school to stream the students into two groups according to their perceived ability in this subject, the performance of each group was also compared. When comparing the number of students who could answer with the proper verb form, the net gain in scores (expressed as a percentage) of the high-score group (43 students) was 11% (57% in the pre-test to 68% in the post-test). The gain in the low-score group (30 students) was 18% (from 18% on the pre-test to 36% on the post-test). The following is an excerpt from a post-lesson interview with a group of students from the low-score group. In the interview, the students were presented with one of the student worksheets which required them to answer questions like "What is he/she?" "What are they?" "What does he/she do?" and "What do they do?"

Researcher 1:   (*showing a student's worksheet*) You have used "he" in your answer to this question and "they" in that question. Why?

Student 1:   (*pointing to the pictures on the worksheet*) Because there is one person here and two there.

… …

Researcher 1:   Can you tell from the statements, instead of the pictures?

Student 2:   (*pointing to the answers in the worksheet*) Here, "he" represents one person, and when there are two people, "they" will be used.

… …

Student 3:   "Are" is also used for plurals.

… …

Researcher 2:   (*pointing to an incorrect answer on the worksheet*) Why is the answer wrong?

Student 2:   Because "s" is missed out [in the verb form].

Researcher 2:   Why is it wrong that "s" is missed out [in the verb form]?

Student 4:   Because [the subject item] refers to one person.

The examples described above suggest that the research lessons, making use of particular patterns of variation focusing on bringing out the critical aspects/features, did bring about a positive effect on the performance of the students in the area concerned. In particular, the performance of the low-score group was encouraging, as they showed no less gain than the high-score group did.

However, caution must be exercised in interpreting the data from the pre- and post-tests. It should be noted that the pre- and post-tests were designed to measure the short-term effect of the research lessons. Our interest is to assess the effect of teaching on student learning, and therefore the post-tests were administered as soon as possible after the lesson, to avoid the result being affected by coaching at home.

It should also be noted that research lessons did not always result in significant improvement in student learning. The reason was that teachers' enactment of the lesson as planned strongly influenced the effectiveness of the research lesson and hence was reflected in student learning. Very often, teachers' enactment of the research lesson deviated from the original plan, owing to the dynamic nature of the classroom situation as well as to teachers' individual differences. This, however, gave us the opportunity for relating the act of teaching to student learning outcomes, which in turn helped us to improve the design of the research lessons. The following is an example that illustrates how patterns of variation enacted in the research lessons affected students' learning outcomes.

Primary 4 Chinese language, "A short pencil"

In this study, one of the objects of learning was the ability to distinguish the subtle difference in meaning and hence proper usage of the synonyms of "take" [拿]: "receive" [接], "fish out" [掏], "carry" [提], "pick up" [撿], "throw" [拋], and "drop" [丟]. Each word has a slightly different meaning associated with some action using the hand. The plan was to help the students discern the subtle difference in meaning between two words that would be used in the same sentence. The sentence pattern would be kept invariant and only the word with the hand radical changed. However, when two of the teachers (A and B) taught the research lesson, they each had a different focus, resulting in different patterns of variation being enacted and different student outcomes in this respect. Teacher A focused on differentiating the semantic meanings of the words in relation to the linguistic context, i.e., the rest of a sentence. In contrast, Teacher B focused on the decontextualized meaning of each word on its own and the action of the hand conveyed by each word. For example, Teacher A asked the students to compare two sentences:

> He *received* the pencil from her hand.
> He *took* the pencil from her hand.

She drew the students' attention to the semantic meaning of the sentence when the word "received" [接] was used — there was an intention to give by the one holding the pencil. "She" is the actor while "he" is the receiver. The word "took" [拿] however, did not convey the same meaning. "He" became the actor.

Teacher B used the following two sentences:

> Don't *drop* banana skins onto the floor.
> Don't *throw* banana skins onto the floor.

Teacher B focused on the action of the hand and asked the students to act out "drop" and "throw." The subsequent discussion also focused on the action of the hand — large movement or small movement, size of swing, and the angle made by the arm.

It would be expected that Teacher A's students should perform better on a question requiring them to fill in seven blanks in a text with the appropriate words (with the hand radical), since Teacher A focused on the semantic instead of decontextualized meanings of the words. The reason is that the test required students to understand the semantic meanings of the words in order to answer the question properly. This was indeed borne out by the results of the post-test. While the number of students who got ALL the words correct increased from two (pre-test) to eighteen (post-test) in Teacher A's class, only six of Teacher B's students got all the words correct in the post-test. Moreover, of the two words [掏] and [提] that both Teacher A and Teacher B gave special attention to in class, all thirty-three students in Teacher A's class were able to fill in these two words correctly. However, in Teacher B's class, less than 60% of the students could get these correct in each case. A more detailed account can be found in Lo et al. (2004) and Lo and Ko (2003).

Teacher empowerment

Some of the participant teachers demonstrated remarkable professional growth over the three years of the project. For instance, one of the Chinese language teachers, having participated in three cycles of Learning Studies in the first year, grasped the idea and put the Theory of Variation into practice with marked improvement in her own teaching as well as in her students' learning outcomes. Thus, in the second year, she was invited to work in the capacity of Teaching Development Consultant of the Centre for the Development of School Partnership and Field Experience of the Hong Kong Institute of Education, to help develop Learning Studies in various primary schools. She was subsequently appointed Primary School Master (Curriculum Development) to a newly established primary school, where she used Learning Study as one of the major means for the school's development. Another three mathematics teachers, who had joined the project at the very beginning and became familiar with the theoretical framework of the project, began to take the lead in running cycles of Learning Studies in the school.

In the following, the results of the analyses drawn from two sets of data, including individual teacher interviews and the researchers' observation made at different stages of the Learning Studies, are presented and discussed.

Analysis of the interview data

In the second (2001–02) and the third (2002–03) years of the study, we interviewed all the teacher participants (a total of 37 and 27 teachers from both schools in the respective year of study) after they had completed the first Learning Study. Of the 27 teachers who were interviewed in the third year, 15 had taken part in at least three Learning Studies and had been interviewed in the previous year. In other words, actually 49 teachers were interviewed. They can be classified into three groups who joined the research project at different times and with different experience in implementing Learning Studies:

- *Group 1*: Teachers who had taken part in one to three Learning Studies by the second year but did not continue in the third year (22 teachers);
- *Group 2*: Teachers who had participated in at least three Learning Studies by the third year (15 teachers) and the analysis was based on the third year interview data;
- *Group 3*: Teachers who had joined the project in the third year and had carried out only one Learning Study (12 teachers).

The interviews were conducted on an individual basis and were aimed at determining: (a) to what extent the teachers agreed that the approach for catering for individual differences used by the project team is useful and they were willing to put it into practice, and (b) how well they understood the conceptual framework of Learning Study (V1, V2 and V3). The interviews were audio-recorded and transcribed verbatim. The result is summarized in the following sections.

Teachers' views of the approach adopted in the study to cater for individual differences

Most of the teachers in the three groups were positive about the usefulness of the approach adopted in the project to cater for individual differences and were willing to use it: about 77% (17/22), 80% (12/15), and 100% (12/12) of the teachers in Groups 1, 2 and 3 respectively. In particular, many of the teachers were confident in the use of the variation in students' thinking and understanding specific subject matter (V1) in helping them to cater for individual differences. This is important because it shows whether the project, which aimed at catering for individual differences through empowering teachers, has been successful. The following are quotes from four teachers:

> To the teacher, it has a big impact ... Before, though I would wonder why they could not understand, I would not try to follow up to find out ... But now we would try to find out where students have difficulties and help them. (LWH TI 0102)

> When I found students with problems, I would ask myself why they made these kinds of mistakes. Maybe ask them to explain and listen to them more. Then I found that I had not spent enough time doing this, to get in touch with children, to listen and to find out what they know, which would affect the group's lesson planning. Because every class is so different ... Then we found out where students are in their understanding and we planned the teaching accordingly. (OMY TI 0102)

> In this project, we began by looking into students' different ways of understanding something. By doing so, we were actually catering for students of different levels of achievement. Students who are low achievers ... are often weak at seeing things in a more comprehensive way. So, if we can show them different ways of thinking, they will be able to view things in a comprehensive manner. And the learning atmosphere will be better when students discover things for themselves rather than have the teacher telling them everything. (TJL TI 0203)

> Before, we believed that students' learning difficulties were due to their innate ability. But after joining a Learning Study, I understand that the greatest impact on students' learning outcomes is in fact our own teaching. In the classroom, we should provide more opportunities for students to enquire and experience the subject matter. When we have found out about students' different ways of understanding the subject matter, we can design

more appropriate learning experiences for them. This can really help to improve the students' learning. (CYH TI 0203)

Teachers' understanding and use of the conceptual framework

1. Variation in students' understanding (V1) and use of diagnostic assessments

Many teachers demonstrated good understanding of how to capitalize on students' different ways of understanding the identified subject matter to cater for individual differences: about 55% (12/22) of the teachers in Group 1, 80% (12/15) in Group 2, and about 67% (8/12) in Group 3. They also understood the function and the value of using diagnostic assessment items that were developed for the pre-tests and post-tests in the Learning Studies. While the former was considered a piece of useful information on the students' difficulties for their lesson planning, the latter was taken as a kind of instant feedback on how well they had implemented the plan and how they could improve on it.

> The pre-test can show students' learning difficulties. … If we focus on their difficulties and find ways to help them to learn, then such a lesson should be suited to the ability of the students. … the results of the post-test can help us to reflect, to see whether our teaching is successful. If we have planned the lesson according to the pre-test results to enhance student learning, then the outcome of the post-test is very important, because it shows how much the students can learn or whether they still have difficulties. It goes beyond this year. It has implications for what I should do in the next year. (LWH TI 0102)

> When we find a problem in student learning in the pre-test, we can focus on dealing with this problem in our teaching. … It (the post-test result) does not only reflect student learning. … It also shows us where we can improve or where students fail to understand certain basic ideas. … The pre-test and post-test are useful because they help us to look at our teaching. Even though it might not be very comprehensive, it is an indicator. (KMY TI 0102)

> We chose a certain topic, then we focused on that specific topic in setting the pre-test, the purpose of which was not for assigning marks to students but for collecting information (about students' understanding of the topic) … this was different from our practices in the past. But setting pre-tests is quite a difficult job. (WWY TI 0203)

The teachers also became better at setting test items to find out about students' prior knowledge, the different ways in which students may interpret the same phenomenon, and the difficulties that they may encounter. The teachers were more serious about setting the pre-test and would dedicate time to design suitable test items and methods for subsequent analysis that could reveal students' different understanding of each critical aspect/feature identified. The following are some examples of good test items:

(a) Having identified the use of the combinations of "10" as a critical aspect for the Primary 1 students to learn to solve double-digit subtraction tasks that involve re-grouping (e.g., "11–7"), a pre-test question was set to measure their inclination towards the use of the combinations of "10" in addition. In this question, the students were asked to do a number of calculations. Each one involved calculating the sum of three single-digit numbers given in a box, two of which will add up to "10" (see below). As well as writing down the answer, the students were required to circle the two numbers that they would add up first, so that we could trace their inclination in making use of the combinations of "10" in calculations.

Calculate the sum of the three numbers given in the box, and circle the two numbers that you add up first.

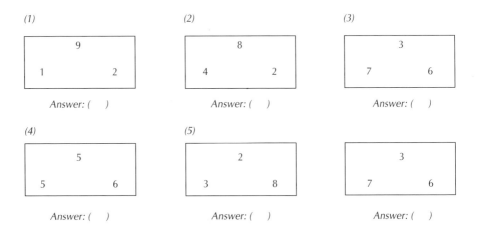

(1)
9	
1	2

Answer: (   )

(2)
8	
4	2

Answer: (   )

(3)
3	
7	6

Answer: (   )

(4)
5	
5	6

Answer: (   )

(5)
2	
3	8

Answer: (   )

3	
7	6

Answer: (   )

(b) In another Learning Study, P3 general studies "the colour of light," to find out whether students had the concept that white light is composed of different colours of light, and so can be split up to show a rainbow, two questions were set to test students' understanding (refer to the diagram below).

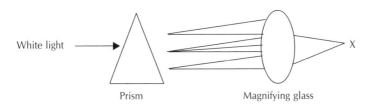

White light   Prism   Magnifying glass   X

In the first question, students were asked to indicate the colour of the light at X. This was to test whether they would be able to deduce that since a rainbow is formed by splitting up white light into its component colours, recombining the different colours of light using a magnifying glass (focusing to a point) should result in white light.

The second question was set to find the different levels of students' understanding of this concept:

If the white light (in the diagram) is replaced by a ray of red light, which of the following will be seen coming out of the prism (please circle the correct answer)?

(*i*)   *A rainbow.*
(*ii*) *A rainbow that has turned red.*
(*iii*) *Only the red part of the original rainbow.*
(*iv*) *Other. Please explain with a diagram.*

If option (i) was chosen, then the students showed little understanding of the relation between white light and the rainbow. If option (ii) was chosen, then at least the students understood that since the other components of white light were absent, it would not be possible to see the other colours of the rainbow. If option (iii) was chosen, then the students truly understood that, when white light was split up into its component colours, the different coloured lights would take up different positions in the rainbow. This also shows that these students knew that, when the colour components other than red were absent, the red light passing through the prism would not spread to take up space originally occupied by other colour components.

(c) A Primary 6 Chinese language study group decided to build on the studies conducted in the previous years to enhance students' capability to appreciate and hence use appropriate and creative similes in writing. One of the critical aspects identified concerns the structure of a simile, and another the appropriateness of the simile used to describe certain objects. Therefore, a pre-test question was set to tap students' prior understanding in these respects. In this question, students were to:
(i)   identify from a text the sentences that have used similes;
(ii) analyse the structure of the simile used for each sentence identified in (i); and
(iii) indicate if any of the sentences identified in (i) uses the simile inappropriately, and rewrite it in an appropriate way.

Whereas (i) and (ii) measured whether the students were familiar with a simile and its structure, (iii) provided information on whether the students were aware that simile should be used appropriately and if they were able to write a simile appropriately.

2.   Variation in teachers' ways of handling the object of learning (V2)

Apart from being sensitized to students' different ways of understanding, the teachers, in planning a research lesson, started by looking for a worthwhile object of learning, identifying its critical aspects, and trying to use variation to show the critical aspects instead of merely focusing on the activities, the kinds of approach, and teaching aids. This had become a routine. Many teachers believed that the collaboration among teachers who had different ways of handling the identified object of learning could help them teach better: 50% (11/22) of the teachers in Group 1, about 47% (7/15) in Group 2, and about 67% (8/12) in Group 3. They were also able to improve on the lesson plan as well as their own practice, through peer classroom observations and the mutual sharing in the pre- and post-lesson conferences.

> In research meetings, we focus on discussing the critical aspects of a particular (object of learning on a) topic. ... Based on our findings on student difficulties, we made adjustments in defining the critical aspects or teaching objectives. (KMY TI 0102)

> How we understood "student-centred" in the past was rather simple: "Would students be able to understand it if I put it this way?" That's all we considered. We did not pay attention to empowering students to find out why things happen or to get the gist of what they are learning in their learning process ... However, what we have achieved in these several research lessons is that we were able to approach the topic in a clear and specific way, unlike what we did in the past. Previously, we only set the teaching objective in a broad and general sense, for example, how to develop students' generic skills, how to develop students' ... learning. (CTF TI 0203)

> One person's wisdom is limited. What you can consider will not be able to exhaust all the students' problems. If different teachers try to find out what difficulties their students will encounter, make use of their collective wisdom, then find ways to deal with it, I find that this is very helpful from the perspectives of both the students and teachers. (IMK TI 0203)

3.   Using variation as a guiding principle of pedagogical design (V3)

Unlike the notions of V1 and V2, relatively fewer teachers showed good understanding of how patterns of variation (i.e., V3) can help to facilitate students to discern the identified object of learning by focusing their attention on the critical aspects/features: 0% (0/22) in Group 1, about 27% (4/15) in Group 2, and about 17% (2/12) in Group 3. These teachers were also able to decide what patterns of variation were appropriate for bringing about the learning of specific objects of learning and to present those patterns through various learning activities.

> I think it (i.e., the conceptual framework of the project) is really useful. We did think of V1 and V2 before [joining the project], and so we can easily

become totally involved in these. However, we seldom ... or even never thought of V3 ... This time, when we did it, we would think: there are so many variations ... How do we find the critical aspects? Before, we did not know that we could find the critical aspects from the variations in students' understanding of the subject matter. Also, there is a great difference between finding these critical aspects from students, and telling students what we imposed on them. (CTF TI 0203)

The Theory of Variation not only enables us to look at the problem from different perspectives, but both students and teachers can make use of variation to examine a particular topic. For example, squashing a rectangle changes it into a parallelogram. We can compare the variations in the diagrams: similarities and differences in properties. This theory can be put into practice in different subjects. It's only a question of whether you do it consciously or subconsciously. If you do it consciously, you will strengthen your use of it and be able to apply it a bit more thoroughly. (CLP TI 0203)

Of those teachers who had difficulty grasping the idea of using patterns of variation in planning a lesson, some may also have reservations about its usefulness in catering for individual differences. The following teacher, for example, was not very clear about what to vary and what to keep invariant. She confused the pattern of variation with variation in teaching strategies.

In fact I do not really know if I have understood this theory very well, but I tried to teach using different methods. First I may let the children talk about it, then turn the words into writing, then express it in different tones. Anyway, using different methods to show the same thing. Although I am not very sure if it is right, I still would try it out. (LPC 0102)

4.   Summary: what do we learn from the interview data?

The results above suggest that the majority of teachers in all three groups had good faith of the study's approach in helping them cater for individual differences. However, two major findings emerged when we tried to compare the percentages between groups of teachers as regards their understanding of the conceptual framework by the year of study in which the teachers were interviewed. One of the comparisons was made between Group 1, which consisted of teachers having participated in one to three cycles of Learning Study by the second year, and Groups 2 and 3, which were composed of teachers who had participated in one to three or more cycles of Learning Study by the third year. Higher percentages of teachers who could demonstrate a good understanding of the conceptual framework were observed in Groups 2 and 3. This may be due to the fact that the methodology of Learning Study had been fine-tuned in the third year of the project, following the modifications made in the second year, thus providing a better foundation for the newly participating teachers to grasp the methodology quickly and for the experienced ones to develop in the use of it.

Another comparison was made between Group 2 and Group 3. Although both groups were interviewed in the third year of the project, they differed in experience of implementing Learning Study: teachers in Group 2 had conducted three or more cycles of Learning Study and those in Group 3 one cycle of Learning Study. Given the same well-defined methodology, it seems natural to expect that the more experience the teachers had in running Learning Study, the more quickly they would learn and master the conceptual framework. This has been shown by the higher percentages of teachers in Group 2 who had good understanding of V1 and V3. However, the percentage of teachers in the more experienced group who showed a good understanding of V2 was lower than that in the newly participating group. This may indicate that there are factors hindering the teachers from collaborating with each other (the very essence of V2). These factors have yet to be explored (see the section "Factors contributing to or hindering the project's implementation", pp. 71–73) and addressed by further refinement of the methodology.

Triangulation with researchers' observation

Apart from the interview data, the researchers, who had been in collaboration with the teachers throughout the Learning Studies, made observations on the teachers' progresses as regards different aspects of their professional development (such as their knowledge about their students, their subject knowledge, their teaching practice, etc). The information below draws on the observation data and summarizes a number of ways in which we found that some teachers were becoming more competent and confident in their teaching.

They gained better knowledge of their students' potential abilities.

The focus on V1 helped the teachers to know more about their students' preconceptions and difficulties. For example, one of the mathematics teachers, who had been following the project since it began, did not believe at the beginning that her class could benefit from discussions as opposed to direct instructions. She thought that her students were low in ability and it would take too long in class and so it would not be practical. However, in the research lesson on "prisms," she made her first attempt to discuss with her class the ways they would define the properties of prisms. She was amazed that her class could actually come up with those properties themselves through discussion. She also found that it was much easier for her to provide feedback and to clarify their misconceptions. As she revealed in an evaluation meeting held at the school, by knowing more about her students, she was now much more confident in her teaching.

They developed a better understanding of the subjects they taught.

The focus on identifying worthwhile objects of learning and searching for the corresponding critical aspects/features helped the teachers to gain deeper understanding of their subject. For example, in a Primary 4 general studies Learning Study on "electric current" carried out in the third year, one of the teachers was initially worried about her own subject knowledge. As she mentioned in the interview,

> Actually I had a lot of things that I did not know (about the topic "electric current") because I majored in arts, not science. ... but after several meetings, I began to understand what was critical to the learning of the topic ("electric current").

Benefiting from the fact that she was the last one in the group to teach, and so was able to observe others' teaching and then modify the lesson plan, she was actually able to teach with much greater confidence and clarity.

They were willing to exercise professional judgement to adjust (or even to modify) the intended lesson plan in order to accommodate students' variation in understanding during the lesson.

For example, in planning for a Primary 6 mathematics research lesson on "speed," one of the teachers, who taught the class with better academic performance, thought that her students would be able to grasp the concept of "speed" and hence the formula in no more than half of a double lesson dedicated to the research lesson. Therefore, she was prepared to focus the second half of the double lesson on developing a more difficult concept, "average speed." However, when she found that the lesson was progressing more slowly than expected because many students could attain only a partial understanding of the concept of "speed," instead of going ahead with what she had prepared for the lesson, she actually spent the time discussing with the students what their problems were.

They gained confidence in tailoring the curriculum.

Instead of relying on textbooks and feeling that they were constrained by a syllabus or teaching schedules, many teachers were able to break through these constraints and take responsibility for making decisions about the objects of learning that they thought were worthwhile. More importantly, the teachers did not take the prescribed curriculum and implement it without thinking about the continuity of the students' learning experience and whether critical aspects/features essential for the students to learn the topic were included. In other words, the teachers were able to ask critical questions and move beyond what the textbook presented, to focus on the object of learning with the aim of maximizing learning and deepening understanding. They also recognized the importance of tailoring the curriculum to facilitate better learning.

> When we receive a curriculum, we should consider it very carefully. In any dimension of a subject, where is the continuity? … Teachers have to find out the students' prior knowledge. If they do not have a solid foundation, they cannot construct new knowledge . … I also found that the prescribed curriculum sometimes misses out the critical aspects/features. For example, in the teaching of fractions, the curriculum guide made no reference to the concept of "unit and unitizing" … After we completed the research lesson, the students had a better grasp of the concept of "unit." When I taught multiplication and division of fractions in P5, I was able to save a lot of time. (OMY TI 0102)

> My confidence in teaching is increasing. In fact, when I have a better idea of the critical aspects/features of a topic, I become less reliant on the textbook. … And I become more sensitive to how students learn. (CYP TI 0102)

They gained experience in being action researchers.

Having been involved in at least one cycle of Learning Study, most teachers appreciated having an opportunity to work with one another in designing what and how to teach in certain topics. Not only did they believe that they could benefit by focusing the discussion on the object of learning and its critical aspects but also by reflecting on their own practice while sharing with one another and observing others teach.

> This is certainly a kind of teacher professional development … If we do not get together to discuss a topic so seriously, then we usually follow traditional teaching methods. Especially after teaching for so many years, we tend to follow a fixed routine. … While discussing how students learn, it is actually a reflection for teachers … I believe that this is the power of group work, and lots of traditional and new ideas came about when we worked together. (LWH TI 0102)

> What I liked the most is to discover the critical features for a specific topic we picked. For example, we talked about the horizontal cross-section. We came up with several questions … very interesting. … Would it still be the same if it were curved? All cross-sections should be the same. We seldom thought of these issues if they were not raised in the meetings. (NKM TI 0102)

Some teachers have moved into the role of teacher-researcher. This is expressed very well by the following teacher:

> This project has led us to another realm: we no longer just concentrate on teaching and learning. Rather, we have moved into the realm of doing

research. Lastly, I realize that we teachers have undergone a big change: we
have become accustomed to peer observation and peer evaluation. This, in
fact, was another product of running this project. Since the teaching
materials had been developed by the whole team, we did not feel anxious
when we used them to teach. Instead, we were eager to find better ways to
improve our teaching methods. This has been a big step forward in
upgrading our professionalism. (CTF TI 0203)

Being able to observe other teachers teaching the lesson in the Learning
Study was seen as another useful way to improve the lesson, as it offered the
observing teachers a chance to modify the lesson plan.

> Formerly, we only observed our students and only our students could see
> what we were doing. But now we have had the chance to observe other
> teachers employing different teaching methods … We can share our views
> on various ways of teaching. Also, when you (the researcher) come to observe
> us, you can also give us some suggestions. This, of course, will, to a certain
> extent, help to increase our professionalism. (MPY TI 0203)

> We could see if the lesson plan we came up with was practical. Actually, we
> designed the lesson plan together, and so we all decided to teach this way.
> After we observed some problems [in the first trial], we could think of ways
> to solve them immediately. … This would be improving the lesson plan to
> match the reality in the classroom. (CYY TI 0102)

> Actually, this was a golden opportunity to learn from other teachers'
> experience. This kind of experience is so precious because even if you can
> view the video, even if the lecturers themselves come to teach you, you won't
> be able to learn as much. The reason is that, in this project, we not only saw
> first-hand how others teach, but we could also observe how different teachers
> teach the very same topic. Because of this, we could implement what we had
> observed by adapting our own teaching methods right away. By doing so,
> we could learn much more effectively. (LYM TI 0203)

> After working out a teaching plan with other teachers collaboratively, my
> confidence was greatly boosted. After the first lesson was taught, all the
> teachers observed it and then immediately met to discuss plans for
> modifications. We were not satisfied with the teaching plans until we had
> revised it for the third time. It's really good that we had this chance to adjust
> our plans. (TJL TI 0203)

They contributed to professional activities in public seminars.

A number of teachers who captured the essence of Learning Study emerged
as leaders in the team. Some of them started to lead other teams of teachers
in the school to conduct Learning Studies. Many of the teachers also presented
their studies in seminars to an audience of teachers and principals of other
schools. They were able to articulate the theoretical framework of the study
and presented an analytic account of their research lessons. And by so doing,

they gained more insights into what they have been doing within the project.

> Before going to the seminars, we have to think about how we planned the
> lesson and what we found in the evaluation many, many times. And each
> time we thought about it, we would be more familiar with it. I think this is
> one way to push yourself to reflect on what you have done. And each time
> you reflect, you would know more. It doesn't hurt to reflect more; from the
> teachers' perspective, it is better to attend seminars on teaching and learning,
> rather than those on curriculum reforms, which are so boring. (CYH TI
> 0102)

> It would help us to be more familiar with the project. If we are not familiar
> with it, how could we talk to others about it? You cannot expect people only
> to praise you; some people might argue with you. Therefore, you first have
> to believe in the project before you can introduce it to others. (NKM TI
> 0102)

School development

In this section, the written comments from the school principals and teachers
were mainly used to describe the development of the two participant schools
over the three years, and their future adoption of Learning Study.

Schools' development over the past three years

Alongside the development of the project, a more collaborative working
culture among teachers has emerged in the two partnership schools. Learning
Study was also regarded as a powerful way of enhancing teachers' professional
development, and in particular, in finding ways to help students of different
abilities learn better, by focusing on what students might have difficulty in
learning in certain topics and how to teach these topics effectively. The
following are excerpts from the school principals' written remarks on
participating in the project:

> Our Project, "Catering for individual differences — building on variation,"
> is a research-based project. Different subjects have their own lesson
> preparation group which meets regularly to discuss issues like setting learning
> targets, anticipating student difficulties, and experimenting with various
> teaching methods. All this is done to ensure a high quality of teaching. The
> lesson preparation groups, peer collaboration, and observation, and post-
> teaching analysis and reflections, all help to enhance our teachers'
> confidence and professionalism. At the same time, our school has also
> developed into a learning organization that is vibrant with the culture of
> innovation and peer collaboration. (ISB Sch1 0203)

This project widened the view of our teachers in seeing "individual differences" not only in ability but also in students' different ways of experiencing and understanding the world. This gives teachers a sense of success and satisfaction. But, it did take time and effort for teachers to learn to identify the critical aspects of the chosen objects of learning and to use variation in lesson design. However, when teachers saw that students, one by one, group by group, could grasp the object of learning, they were so happy that they forgot about the weariness. Also, when teachers took part in the post-lesson evaluation, analysis, and lesson modification, they were undoubtedly behaving in a professional way. Moreover, the lessons were so carefully and systematically structured to highlight the critical aspects of the identified object of learning that they were full of joy from students' happiness at being able to learn. This has led to the narrowing of the differences in students' learning outcomes, and students' various potential being maximized. (LKH Sch2 0203)

Schools' future adoption of Learning Study

Learning Study has been adopted by both schools as one of the major means to develop school-based curricula and to nurture a critical mass of teacher leaders. One of the schools has also successfully applied for the Quality Education Fund to support Learning Studies to be conducted in various subjects (2003–04), and continues to take part in the seed project of the Curriculum Development Institute. The second school is also actively working on a similar proposal to the Quality Education Fund to develop and support Learning Study. The following are excerpts from the school principals' written remarks on their plans to continue the development of Learning Studies in their schools:

> To consolidate the foundation of the school curriculum developed during the past three years, we will carry out a project entitled "Sharing the culture of Learning Study" in 2003. In collaboration with CDSPFE of the Hong Kong Institute of Education, we will vigorously conduct Learning Studies to transform teachers into a team of learning-minded teaching staff. In the coming year, all the teachers will actively help to develop a culture in the school where teachers collaborate with each other, the consultant is working as their friend, and teachers are exchanging views about teaching. We also want to develop effective teaching methods to enhance students' interest in learning and their learning outcomes. Through developing a network of schools, we hope that teachers from different schools will share their practical experience in curriculum development in their own schools. It is also hoped that a culture of research on teaching will be promoted. (ISB Sch1 0203)

> It was three years ago when education reform was about to begin that the whole school voted to participate in this project. It is often remarked that education reform can bring about school development. But I would say it is

Learning Study that nurtures the school's culture, helps teachers to design curriculum, offers an opportunity for teachers' professional development, and provides a blueprint for the school's curriculum reform. Nowadays, as education reforms are launched vigorously, our teachers have already grasped the pedagogy of variation, which was demonstrated to be useful and effective in enhancing student learning. We will continue to treat this as a major item for school development. (NWL Sch2 0203)

Establishing a professional knowledge base of teaching is also what the teachers in both schools are planning to do, on the basis of the Learning Studies that were conducted over the past three years. To the teachers, it is very important that they can build on what they have done, to be able to plan for a coherent and meaningful curriculum in an effective manner:

It would be far better if there were some references we could look for while doing the study. I mean it would be even better if we could refer to colleagues' previous experiences so that we do not need to start from zero every time. The information collected can also inform us on how to adjust the curriculum at a macro level, say from Primary 1 to 3. (WWY TI 0203)

I think time for initiating is very important. We also need to establish a database. Information has to be stored after all, and it would be time-consuming and ineffective if we need to set the pre-test and post-test all over again every time. (CTF TI 0203)

Dissemination activities and their impact

Since 2000, members of the research team have been participating in seminars, workshops, and conferences to explain the use of the conceptual framework for improving classroom teaching and learning, as well as to share our experiences of carrying out Learning Studies. A summary of the seminars/workshops/conferences which members took part in up to August 2003 is provided in Appendix 2. A list of publications published under the project in various contexts is also provided in Appendix 3.

Learning Studies were also developed by another 42 primary schools, which participated in the Progressive and Innovative Primary School (PIPS) project of the Hong Kong Institute of Education, in Chinese language, English language, mathematics, general studies, and art in the academic years 2001/02 and 2002/03.

From 2003/04 onwards, Learning Studies have been carried out in five Key Learning Areas at secondary level: mathematics, science, technology, physical education, and arts, through the Quality Education Fund supported Secondary Teaching, Evaluation and Mentoring Project (STEM) of the Hong Kong Institute of Education. A total of 120 Learning Studies at both primary and secondary levels will also be conducted through another government-supported research project, "Variation for the Improvement of Teaching and Learning" (2004–07), of the Hong Kong Institute of Education.

Factors contributing to or hindering the project's implementation

Group dynamic

Most of the Learning Study groups set up within the project were quite successful. They had the following characteristics: mutual trust between the teachers and researchers, and good and open communication between the two parties. There were more contributing members in the group, who took the initiative in designing teaching tools and coming up with suggested lesson plans. All members worked together in a collegial and positive atmosphere. Some members had successful experiences in conducting research lessons.

The less successful Learning Study groups (three out of thirteen groups, two in the first year and one in the second year) had the following characteristics: teachers were not enthusiastic about being members, and they were told to take part by the senior management. There was no rapport between the teachers and the researchers, and the teachers did not understand the purpose of the project. There was little involvement of the panel chair and members of the senior management in the Learning Study group itself; thus, the senior management of the school did not fully understand the needs of the participating teachers and so were not able to make appropriate and efficient arrangements to facilitate the project accordingly. When this happened, the participation of some teachers in the Learning Study became minimal. They were unwilling to give the time that was required for consensus building and in-depth analysis of the object of learning. In some cases, the teachers could not even agree on a lesson plan, so two different lesson plans were implemented. In these cases, the quality of the research lesson was compromised.

Institutional factors

Involvement in innovations is, however, only a catalyst for any change to take place in schools. A school environment that is supportive and collegial is also a critical contributing factor to the development of a school culture that would enable the project to take root and flourish. Support from school principals and panel chairs is definitely one of the crucial factors. For instance, when the school principal and the panel chairs knew more about the working details of the project, they were in a better position to make arrangements to facilitate the progress of the project, such as adjusting the timetable so that the same group of teachers could be free for the same period for discussions.

External support

The tripartite collaboration among the schools, the Curriculum Development Institute, and the research team was considered a win-win option for all parties involved, as each benefited in one way or another. For the schools, apart from having financial support, the participant teachers valued the input from the research team and the representative of the Curriculum Development Institute, who had better access to the research literature and teaching resources:

> Our way of thinking about how to teach is different from before, because of the presence of the subject experts. We will think in a wider perspective and go deeper into the subject matter, comparatively speaking. Since the experts will consider the coherence of the whole curriculum, they will think of what we actually need in order to handle a topic without necessarily following the suggestions in the textbook. (WWY TI 0203)

> It is most impressive that the academics are familiar with the research in science. So, it's a lot easier for them to identify the problems than for us. Their opinions are good and inspiring. Take the topic of "Electricity" as an example. We would not have considered teaching in such a great depth had we not participated in the research lesson. I did not even understand the content myself. (CYY TI 0203)

Research service support from the research team was also seen as important by the participant teachers, who were beginning to grasp ways to analyse student data differently from their usual practice.

> We are not experts in processing and analysing students' data. But we were lucky to have the research team supporting us this time. We did not need to worry about this. Of course, should teachers develop this kind of capability as part of their long-term professional development? The answer is definitely "yes." But we need to spend more time on it. So, in the transitional stage, the guidance, analysis and advice provided by the research team is very constructive. (CTF TI 0203)

The representative of the Curriculum Development Institute, as a participant of the study, also felt that the tripartite collaboration maximizes the pooling of expertise and knowledge. The significant findings obtained jointly were also taken as not only being able to inform practice in schools but also contribute to the enhancement of quality education.

> During these three years, I gained fruitful experience from my involvement in the studies. Through sharing with the teachers and the research team, I learnt to be more open to different views and ideas, which I treasured as enrichment for my professional development. Students' feedback also made

me aware of their perspectives on learning a particular topic which, I believe, should be valued by curriculum developers and teachers in planning curriculum. In particular, I admired the team spirit of the teachers and the research team in their pursuit of quality learning and teaching. (WSYJ CDI 0203)

As for the research team, we not only learnt from the tripartite collaboration how the Theory of Variation could be put into practice at different levels; we also learnt from the students what was really critical for their learning of certain topics.

Summary

In this chapter, we described how the theoretical framework of the project was implemented in two schools and illustrated how it worked, from the perspective of the learners, to cater for individual differences in learning in the following ways:

- Improving curriculum by identifying objects of learning which are most worthwhile for students, and the aspects/features associated with those objects of learning which are critical for the students of different needs to grasp them;
- Helping every child to acquire the critical aspects by studying how these can be taught and learnt well, and thus enabling further learning to take place;
- Establishing a professional knowledge base of teaching that informs curriculum development across years and across grade levels, which facilitates coherent and meaningful learning;
- Enhancing teachers' understanding of students as well as their subject knowledge through engaging in Learning Study cycles;
- Increasing teachers' sensitivity in bringing about the intended learning outcomes by supporting teachers' collaboration and lesson observation in using pattern(s) of variation (V3) that take into account the variation in students' understanding of the subject matter (V1), and in teachers' ways of handling the object of learning (V2);
- Developing teachers' capability in using diagnostic assessment to find out the learning difficulties or needs that their students might have in learning particular content;
- Providing teachers with an alternative view of how students learn and what causes differences in students' learning outcomes, which helps them focus on the object of learning and how to structure relevant experiences, thus allowing learning to take place.

In Chapter 5, we illustrate with two cases, one from each of the two partnership schools, how the Learning Studies were carried out.

5

Two Learning Studies

LO Mun Ling, Priscilla LO-FU Yin Wah, Pakey CHIK Pui Man, and PANG Ming Fai

Introduction

Two Learning Studies, one from each of the two partnership schools, are reported in this chapter. The Learning Study reports are mainly descriptive accounts which show the struggles and processes that the research team went through with the teachers in using the theory (explained in Chapter 2) to plan and implement their research lessons, in order to help students of various abilities learn more efficiently.

The Learning Studies reported here, both of which were carried out in the third year of the project, serve as examples to illustrate what Learning Studies are like in practice.

As teacher educators, we have our views on teaching and how students learn and would very much like the research lessons to be carried out in ways that are close to our ways of thinking. However, we also believe that teachers have to experience the learning process themselves, if they are to be in a better position to help students learn. Only when the teachers were comfortable with the actions they were to take, and had true ownership of the research lessons, were they genuinely able to learn and benefit from the Learning Studies. Sometimes what, in our opinion, appeared to be small steps taken by the teachers were in fact courageous attempts by them to taking the beginning of a big step.

The interesting thing about Learning Study is that we did not have an answer to start with. We did not have a ready script for the teachers to act out, nor did we impose our ideas on them. The research lesson that emerged in the end was often the outcome of a process of negotiation, which did not always result in what we would consider to be the best solution in achieving the intended learning outcomes. A research lesson is valuable in the sense that it gives us the opportunity to learn: students, teachers, and researchers all learn during the process. Very often, we had to make compromises, but we gained many insights about how to facilitate teachers' professional development, how to improve the curriculum, and how to help our students learn more effectively.

Some readers may be critical of some of the practices described in these reports, probably on very good grounds, too, because these research lessons are, after all, not "model lessons." Nor have we ever tried to make such a claim. Therefore, when people read about these Learning Studies, we hope that they will approach them from the perspective that these are "research lessons." They represent the genuine and honest attempts of the teachers to improve the learning of their students. These lessons are not an end in themselves, but they contribute to the next cycle of research lessons, which will be better versions than those before them.

Primary 4 General Studies: Electricity

(LO Mun Ling, Priscilla LO-FU Yin Wah, Pakey CHIK Pui Man)

This Learning Study was carried out in School 1 during the third year of the project, when the methodology was better developed and more conscious effort was put into modifying each cycle of the research lesson.

The Learning Study group was made up of three general studies teachers and four research team members. None of the teachers had a strong background in science. Only one teacher had taken science in his senior secondary schooling. Nineteen meetings (including three post-lesson conferences) were held in the period between September 2003 to April 2004.

Stage I: Incubation of ideas

Choosing and defining the object(s) of learning

According to the school's teaching schedule, the research lesson fell into the period when the topic "electricity" would be taught. Reference was then made to the school's textbook and the research literature to find out what is worth learning about electricity at this stage and the likely difficulties that students would encounter. In the textbook, there is a unit, "Electricity and Life," which describes facts of various daily-life phenomena related to electricity and safety in using it. As the information is mainly factual, it would not be sufficient to help the students gain a conceptual understanding of electricity. Since the teachers felt that their students tended to think of science as abstract rather than as close to their daily encounters, the group decided that they would like to choose a topic in electricity that would allow the students to have hands-on experience. As some students had expressed a curiosity about current electricity (e.g., short circuits, light bulbs), the group decided that the research lesson should involve the students investigating how they could light up a bulb using a battery. All students should have had the experience of putting a battery into a torch to make the torch light up, or into their toys to make them work. However, in so doing, they tended to take for granted the circuitry of the appliances. Similarly, they might see their parents putting a light bulb into a lamp stand and switching on the lamp, but they had no idea how a light bulb is actually connected to the circuit through the stand. With this consensus, the object of learning was tentatively narrowed down to the conceptual understanding of "electric current in a circuit." Some of the teachers also pointed out that, once they sparked students' interest in doing experiments with electricity, it was important to deal with safety in using electricity to safeguard against students doing experiments at home using the AC supply.

Identifying critical aspects/features for learning

There have been over a hundred studies on students' conceptions about electricity (Duit and Treagust, 1995; Tasker and Osborne, 1990; Shipstone, 1993; Koumaras et al., 1997; Metioui et al., 1996). These studies indicate four models of students' understanding of how an electric current works in electric circuits: the unipolar model, the clashing current model, the current consumer model, and the scientist's model (Pardhan and Bano, 2001, 302–3).

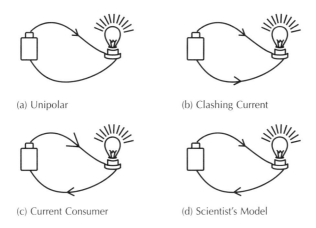

(a) Unipolar   (b) Clashing Current

(c) Current Consumer   (d) Scientist's Model

Figure 5.1 Four models of students' understanding of electric current in a circuit

Another common conception found is that the battery is in general considered a source of current, and it is believed that the current is consumed by the components in the circuit and is not conserved.

A pre-test was designed to gather information on the students' prior knowledge and their different ways of understanding electric current in a circuit. The data collected were then analysed to locate possible difficulties that the students might encounter in learning this topic.

A pilot test was given to a sample of eight P3 and P5 students. The purpose of using P3 students was to find out about students' prior knowledge on this topic. The purpose of using P5 students, who had already been taught this topic, was to reveal persistent preconceptions and possible difficulties that presented themselves as obstacles for learning. Based on their responses, the questions were refined. The final pre-test was administered to ninety-one P4 students. The results are summarized as follows:

- The students' understanding of electric circuits was probed by a question that required them to choose from a number of circuit diagrams the ones that would cause a bulb to light up. Of the 91 students, 37 chose the correct answers; 22 chose circuits that caused a short circuit; 10 chose only circuits that were open (conforming to the unipolar model); 3 chose both open and closed circuits; and 19 did not attempt the question. This means that about 59 (i.e., 37 + 22) students had some idea that a closed circuit was needed for a current to flow, and at least 13 of them (this could be up to 32, i.e., 10 + 3 + 19) were not aware that a current could not flow in an open circuit.

- Interviews with students revealed that some students believed that the current would become smaller after passing through a light bulb, because some part of the current was used up by the light bulb (conforming to the current consumer model). Therefore, questions were set to probe students' understanding of how a current flows in a circuit. For one question, instead of asking the question directly, we decided to make use of some metaphors and asked the students to judge whether the metaphors were appropriate when used to describe how an electric current flows in a circuit.

A number of metaphors were given, and the students were asked to choose the most appropriate one to describe the flow of an electric current in a closed circuit made up of a battery and a light bulb.

In the diagram on your right, if the flow of an electric current is compared to a bus filled with passengers driving from location A to location B, which of the following metaphor(s) do you think can best illustrate the flow of an electric current?

1. A bus filled with passengers departs from location A and heads for the lamp; another bus filled with passengers also departs from location B to the same destination.
2. A bus filled with passengers departs from location A. When it passes the lamp, some of the passengers get off, and the bus continues on its way to location B.

3. A bus filled with passengers departs from location A. When it passes the lamp, all the passengers get off, walk around the lamp, and then all of them board the bus again. The bus then continues on its way to location B.
4. A bus filled with passengers departs from location A. When it passes the lamp, all the passengers get off, and the bus stops there.

These options were also illustrated with appropriate diagrams. The possible concepts held by the students as reflected by their choice of metaphor are listed in the table below (reference was also made to the four models indicated by Pardhan and Bano, 2001):

Metaphor	Possible conception held by the students
M1	Electric current can flow from the two poles of the battery towards the lamp in different directions (conforming to the clashing current model).
M2	Electric current flows in one direction in a closed circuit, and it will be consumed by the lamp (conforming to the current consumer model).
M3	Electric current flows through a circuit in one direction and will not be consumed in a closed circuit (conforming to the scientist's model).
M4	Electric current flows in one direction from the battery to the lamp and does not have to flow through a complete circuit (conforming to a unipolar model).

The table below summarizes the options chosen by the students. As shown in the table, it appeared that there were two major misconceptions in the students' minds: electric current in a closed circuit will be consumed (i.e., 50 students held the current consumer model); and an electric current does not have to flow through a complete circuit (i.e., 23 students held the unipolar model).

Metaphor chosen and possible conception held by the students	Number of students selecting the metaphor
M1: Clashing current model	8
M2: Current consumer model	50
M3: Scientist's model	10
M4: Unipolar model	23
Cannot be categorized/did not attempt	21

Note: Some students subscribed to more than one model. The numbers for M1, M2, and M4 include students who subscribed to more than one model. For M3, only those choosing M3 alone are included.

When we look at the metaphors, we see there was certainly room for improvement. For example, a Hong Kong tram moving along a tramline might have been better because the route is fixed. Also, the current in a circuit flows continuously, so a conveyor belt with people standing on it might be a better metaphor than a bus. However, regardless which metaphor or model we use, there are always limitations. While recognizing the limitations of a model or metaphor, we will be happy to use it as long as it serves its purpose well. For example, we still use the Bohr model of an atom in teaching electronic structure at F4, although our understanding of atoms has moved way beyond that. Even with their imperfections, we trusted that these metaphors could give us valuable ideas about the students' different understanding of how a current flows in a circuit.

For triangulation, we set another question that asked the students to compare the size of the current at four positions in a circuit (see below) and to explain the reasons for their answers.

In the diagram below, the electric current flows from A to B. We are to measure and compare the size of the current at points 1, 2, 3 and 4. Do you think the size of the current measured at these 4 points will be the same? Explain your answers.

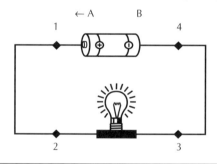

The table on p. 81 summarized the explanations given by the students. Thirty-two students indicated that the size of the current would be the same when measured at the four positions, and two of them provided explanations that conformed to the scientist's model. Fifteen students thought that the size of the current would differ, four of them giving reasons that subscribe to the current consumer model.

- Another question was set to find out whether the students knew that the amount of current could vary depending on the power supply (see the text box below). The students were presented with two circuits (one with only one battery and the other with two batteries in series) and asked to compare the brightness of the light bulbs connected to the two circuits. Of the 91 students, 36 answered that the bulb in the circuit with one battery was dimmer than that in the circuit with two batteries; 24 indicated

	Number of students
Conception shown in the explanations	Pre-test
The size of the current is the SAME at the four positions	
S1: Scientists' model	2
No reason could be provided/no explanation provided	12
Cannot be categorized	18
Sub-total:	**32**
The size of the current is DIFFERENT at the four positions	
D1: Current consumer model	4
No reason could be provided / No explanation provided	4
Cannot be categorized	7
Sub-total:	**15**
Irrelevant/did not attempt	
Sub-total:	**44**
Total:	**91**

that the bulb in the circuit with only one battery was brighter; 16 indicated that the bulbs in both circuits were of the same brightness; and 15 did not attempt the question. This shows that only 36 students knew that the brightness of the bulb is directly related to the number of batteries in series in the circuit.

The light bulb in Diagram 1 is (brighter than/the same in brightness as/dimmer than) that in Diagram 2 in the figure below.

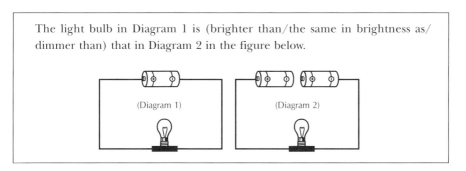

(Diagram 1)   (Diagram 2)

Finalizing the focus of the study

After much deliberation, taking into account the result of the pre-test, the group decided that there should be two objects of learning.

The first object of learning is "the understanding of the flow of an electric current in a closed circuit" and three critical features identified are:
1. An electric current flows in a closed circuit with a battery.
2. An electric current flows in only one direction in a closed circuit and around the complete circuit.

3. The amount of electric current is the same at every point in a closed circuit, and it will not be used up while passing through the circuit.

The second object of learning is "the awareness of safety in the use of electricity" and two critical aspects are:
1. Electric currents can be large or small (i.e., the size aspect).
2. Large electric currents can be dangerous (i.e., the safety aspect).

The concepts involved in some of these critical aspects/features are rather abstract. Some are even metaphorical (e.g., the flow of an electric current). Following a lively discussion regarding the depth of treatment of the lesson, the group came to a consensus that while hands-on activities were to be used to engage students in learning about closed circuits, metaphors could be used to help the students to understand the more abstract concept of how an electric current moves in a circuit.

Stage II: Planning the Lesson

It was decided that the research lesson should utilize a double period (80 minutes). The lesson was to be divided into four major parts, each focusing on one or two critical aspects/features. Patterns of variation needed to help the students discern the critical aspects/features identified were drawn up, and activities were designed to create a meaningful context for learning.

The details of the first lesson plan and the use of variation are as follows:

Part 1: Introduction

*   Give each group of students a magnifying glass to examine the internal structure of a 60W light bulb, in particular, to see which parts of the two ends of the filament are connected. Although the students should be very familiar with light bulbs used at home, they seldom take the trouble to examine the structure closely.
*   Then, show the students a small 15V bulb and ask them to examine the internal structure. The internal structures of the two types of bulb are the same.
*   Focusing on the small 1.5V bulb, ask the students
    a. What will you need in order to light it up?
    b. Can I light up the bulb without any batteries? Why/why not?
    c. How would you use these components (pieces of wire and a battery) to light up the bulb?

Note: Instead of having the students put a battery into a torch to make the torch light up, which was closer to their daily life experience (as mentioned earlier), a bulb and a battery were chosen as the focus. By doing away with the torch or the stand, it was hoped that the students' attention could be focused on the circuit that was made up of the light bulb, the battery, and some pieces of wire. In this experiment, for safety reasons, a small 1.5V bulb and a 1.5V battery were used instead of the 60W light bulb and the power supply.

- Introduce the next part: Let's do an experiment to explore ways to connect these components (referring to wires and batteries) to the bulb in order to light it up.

Use of Variation:

Invariant	Variation	Critical feature(s) to be discerned
A small 1.5V light bulb connected to two wires	Circuit with a battery lights up. Circuit without a battery does not light up.	A battery is needed for the bulb to light up.

It was decided that a are bulb without a stand should be used in the experiment. The reason is that, having the bulb in a stand and two wires protruding, the combinations available for exploration by the students would be very limited. There would be about six ways of setting up the circuit, and the students could completely ignore the internal structure of the bulb.

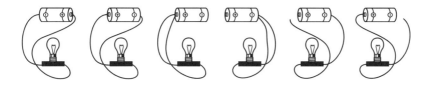

However, using a bare bulb, many more variations are possible; some examples are shown below. The internal structure of the light bulb contributes to variations in the formation of closed circuits since it makes a difference whether the wire is connected to the metal ring or to the base contact.

Source: Stepans, J. (1994). *Targeting students' science misconceptions: Physical science activities using the conceptual change model.* Riverview FL: Idea Factory, Inc., p. 215.

Part 2: Group experiment — setting up a circuit to light up a bulb

- Demonstrate how to do the experiment: try out one or two ways of connecting the given components, draw each circuit on a piece of paper, and record whether it could light up the bulb.
- Let the students work in groups, testing out different circuits using a small 1.5V bulb, a battery, and pieces of wire. They should also record their circuits on paper.
- After the experiment, ask each group of students to put up the drawings of their circuits on two sides of the board: circuits in which the bulb lit up on one side, and circuits in which the bulb did not light up on the other side.
- Discuss with the whole class:
  a. What are the differences between the drawings in these two parts?
  b. What conclusions can we draw?
- To further reinforce the idea of closed circuits, the teacher will demonstrate the following experiment: connect a large light bulb (60W) to a lamp stand plugged into the power socket. The bulb is lit up. Connect a similar bulb (the filament of which has been burnt) to the same lamp stand plugged into the power socket. The bulb is not lit up.
- Invite students to examine the filament of the bulb, and describe the difference (the filament of the burnt bulb is broken and the normal one is not).
- Draw the students' attention to the fact that a circuit must be closed in order to light up a bulb, and call it a "closed circuit."

Use of Variation:

Invariant	Variation	Critical feature to be discerned
Components provided for setting up a circuit: a small 1.5 V light bulb, wires, a battery	Different ways to connect up the bulb and the battery. Some can light up a bulb (closed circuits) and some cannot (open circuits).	A circuit should be closed in order to light up a bulb
A lamp stand plugged into the power socket	A normal bulb can light up. One with a broken filament cannot light up.	

Part 3: Using metaphors to illustrate the flow of an electric current in a closed circuit

Teacher explains how a current flows through an electric circuit and then test the students' understanding by means of some metaphors.

- *Activity 1 (Metaphor of circulating many objects)*: Several students sit in a circle. Each of them holds an object (e.g., an orange). Whenever the teacher gives a signal (e.g., patting a student's shoulder), each student will pass his or her object to the one seated on the right and receive the object handed to him or her from the left at the same time.

    In this case, the students represent the wire (or particles/atoms in a wire). The oranges represent electrons. The teacher represents the battery. When the teacher gives a push, the oranges are circulated in one direction. This represents the situation in which the battery provides the driving force for the electrons to move in a given direction, constituting an electric current. However, in the lesson, terms like atoms and electrons will be avoided. The teacher will only point out that the movement of the oranges represents the electric current. The teacher should also draw the students' attention to the fact that the number of oranges circulating is not changed, i.e., the electric current is not consumed when moving round the circuit.

- *Activity 2 (Metaphor of circulating an object)*: Several students sit in a circle. Only one of them holds an object (e.g., an orange). Whenever the teacher gives a signal (e.g., patting a student's shoulder), the student holding an object will pass the object to the student seated on the right.

    This is not a good metaphor, because only one orange is circulated. If this is the case, then the flow of an electric current will not be continuous, and the size of the current will vary at different positions in the circuit at any particular instance.

- *Activity 3 (Metaphor of moving along chairs)*: Several students sit on chairs in a circle. Whenever the teacher gives a signal (e.g., patting a student's shoulder), each student moves to sit on the chair to the right.

    In this case, the chairs represent the wire (or atoms in the wire). Each student represents an electron. When the students move from one chair to another in the same direction, this represents the movement of an electric current. The number of students remains the same, and this represents the fact that an electric current is not consumed when moving round a closed circuit. The signal from the teacher represents the driving force provided by the battery. When the teacher removes one chair from the circle to create a gap, the movement stops because the student who is supposed to move over will have to stop or fall onto the floor since there is no longer a chair. This represents the situation of an open circuit.

- *Activity 4 (Metaphor of domino game)*: The teacher shows a video about a domino game. Some domino pieces are arranged in a circle. One of them is pushed down by a finger, which causes the others to fall one after the other.

  In this case, the finger represents a battery, giving a driving force. The domino pieces represent the wire. As the domino pieces fall, the energy is transmitted through the domino pieces like electrical energy is transmitted through the wire. This illustrates the idea of flow; however, it represents only one pass, and because the domino pieces cannot get up by themselves, the process cannot be continuous. Therefore, it is not a good metaphor for the flow of an electric current in a circuit.

  Note: The teachers anticipated that the students would have difficulty arranging the domino pieces without any of them falling down ahead of time. Since the focus was on the interpretation of the metaphor rather than on playing with the dominoes, the teachers decided that they should make a video recording instead of letting the students set up the domino pieces. This would avoid distracting the students from the focus of the lesson.

- *Activity 5 (Metaphor of water pump)*: The teacher shows a video on the operation of a water pump. Two ends of a plastic tube filled with water are connected to a pump. When the pump is turned on, the water in the plastic tube begins to flow through the tube in a continuous way. The students can see that the water circulates continuously in the system, as long as the pump is on.

In this case, the pump represents the battery, the tube represents the wire, and the movement of the water represents the flow of an electric current.

After each of the above activities, there should be a detailed debriefing on each metaphor, focusing on the following points:

a. What/who performs the role of the battery in a closed circuit?
b. What/who performs the role of the wires?
c. Is the metaphor a good one to show the flow of an electric current in a closed circuit?

After all the activities, discuss with the students:

a. What are the differences between these activities?
b. Which activities do you think best illustrate how a closed circuit works? Why?

Use of Variation:

Invariant	Variation	Critical feature(s) to be discerned
Each metaphor is used to describe the flow of an electric current in a closed circuit.	Appropriate or inappropriate illustration of the flow of an electric current in a closed circuit.	a. The flow of an electric current in a closed circuit is continuous. b. The current moves through the complete circuit in the same direction. c. The amount of current in the circuit is the same everywhere and will not be consumed. d. A battery is needed for a current to flow through a circuit.

Part 4: Safety in the use of electricity

- Demonstrate that the current in a circuit increases with the use of more batteries, by noting the brightness of a small 3.8V bulb as the number of batteries increases from one to four. The small bulb will reach its maximum brightness and finally will be burnt.
- Demonstrate that the current produced using four batteries is large enough to cause some fine tungsten wires to burst into flame.
- Demonstrate that this seemingly large current is not yet large enough to light up a 60W light bulb, but the power supply from our wall socket can.
- Help the students to draw the conclusion from the demonstrations above that the current from the power supply must be very large and that large currents can be dangerous and so must be handled with great caution. Students should be discouraged from experimenting with electricity using the power supply at home.

Use of Variation:

Invariant	Variation	Critical aspect(s) to be discerned
A small 3.8V light bulb in a circuit.	The number of batteries connected in series in the circuit. The brightness of the bulb.	An electric current can be large or small. The current becomes larger when more batteries are connected in series.

Invariant	Variation	Critical aspect(s) to be discerned
Some fine tungsten wires in a circuit	The number of batteries connected in series in the circuit. The tungsten wires do or do not burst into flames with different number of batteries.	A large current can cause the tungsten to burst into flames. A large current can be dangerous.
The source of power supply (four batteries)	A 1.5V light bulb (which is lit up) or a 60W light bulb (which is not lit up)	The current needed to light up a 60W bulb is much larger than that produced by four batteries.
A 60W light bulb	The power supply: four batteries, home power supply (220V). Whether the light bulb is lit up (using home power supply) or not (using four batteries).	An electric current produced by the home power supply is much larger than that produced by four batteries. The current produced by the power supply at home can be dangerous.

Stage 3: Implementation of the research lesson

The research lesson (lasting 80 minutes) was implemented in three cycles. In each cycle, one of the three participant teachers taught the research lesson to his or her class while other teachers and the research team members observed. Each cycle of the research lesson was followed by a post-lesson conference in which the group members shared their insights and observations made during the lesson. Some changes made to improve the lesson plan in each cycle were noted as follows:

The first cycle of the research lesson and recommended changes

The lesson was taught according to the lesson plan. Some improvements for the next round of teaching were suggested:
- When dealing with Part 2, group experiment in setting up a closed circuit, it was noticed that the students were still not very clear about the structure of a light bulb. Specifically, they could hardly differentiate between the metal ring and the base contact of the light bulb. This problem was also reflected in the circuits that they drew. Therefore, it was suggested that, after the students had examined the structure of the light bulb, the teacher should summarize on the board the structure of a light bulb, and highlight the three parts: the glass bulb, the metal ring at the base of the glass bulb, and the base contact (see Figure 5.2 on p. 89).

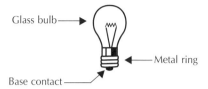

Figure 5.2 The three parts that constitute a light bulb

The teachers should also draw the students' attention to the tungsten filament that was inside the glass bulb. It is this tungsten filament that glows and gives out light. Students should be guided to trace where the two ends of the filaments are connected: one end is connected to the metal ring; the other end is connected to the base contact.

- In Part 3, using metaphors to illustrate the flow of an electric current in a circuit, it was found that one of the activities involving students moving around the chairs was difficult to carry out, due to the limited space available at the front of the classroom. Also, the students did not understand that they had to move from one chair to another in a sitting position without standing up. The teachers felt that there were enough similar metaphors already, so to avoid the confusion caused they decided to cancel this activity in the next round of teaching.

    It was also felt that the debriefing after each activity should be strengthened so that students could understand why some metaphors are appropriate and some are not in describing the flow of an electric current in a circuit.

- It was observed that, while doing the group experiments, some of the students noticed that the wire became hot because they had set up a short circuit. Therefore, it was recommended that the teachers should draw on the students' experience of a short circuit when they dealt with safety in the use of electricity.

The second cycle of the research lesson and recommended changes

- Following the suggestion about clarifying the structure of a light bulb, the teacher used a large 60W light bulb as a teaching aid in her explanation. Despite this, it was found students had difficulty recording the circuit. It was then agreed that the teacher should describe the cross-sectional structure of a light bulb with a diagram (see Figure 5.3) and label the parts, so that students could refer to these when drawing their circuits and during the discussion.

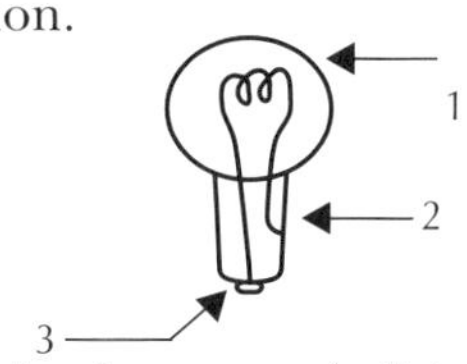

Figure 5.3 The labeled cross-sectional structure of a light bulb recommended for the third cycle

- It was also suggested that, instead of requiring the students to draw the bulb and the cell, which might be quite complicated for them, the teacher could prepare figures of the bulb and cell, so that the students could paste these onto their pieces of paper and then just draw in the wires.
- It was noted that the students were inclined to copy the teacher's demonstration, which was a successful case in lighting up a bulb, and ignored those set-ups that were unsuccessful. It was therefore recommended that the teacher should demonstrate both a successful and an unsuccessful case and remind the students to keep records of all cases that they had tried out, whether successful or not.
- Apart from asking the students to post up their circuit diagrams on the board (those in which the bulb lit up on one side of the board, and those in which the bulb did not light up on another side), it was suggested that the teacher should trace out the path of the current in each circuit with a black felt pen. In this way, the students' attention would be drawn to what was most critical: for those circuits in which the bulb lit up, the current could move through a complete path. In the cases when the bulb did not light up, the path was not closed. It was hoped that this would help the students to discern by themselves that a closed circuit was needed for a current to flow and for the bulb to be lit.
- The debriefing after each activity should be further strengthened, and opportunities should be provided for the students to discuss among themselves whether the metaphors were appropriate in explaining how a current flows. It was important to help the students focus on what the metaphors were meant to represent instead of on the metaphors themselves.

The third cycle of the research lesson and recommended changes

- The lesson was taught according to the revised plan. It was suggested that while highlighting the closed circuits, the teacher might also contrast them with some "open circuits."
- The debriefing after demonstrating the burning of a mass of tungsten wires by four cells needed to be strengthened, to drive home the importance of observing safety precautions in using electricity at home.

Stage 4: Evaluation

Learning outcomes

1.   Comparison between the pre- and post-test results

The teachers administered the post-test, which was parallel to the pre-test, to the same 91 students after their research lessons. The results are summarized as follows:

- In the pre-test, only 37 (about 41%) of the students could correctly identify the closed circuits in which a bulb will light up. In the post-test, 74 (about 81%) could correctly identify the two closed circuits that can light up a bulb among the given four circuits.
- In the post-test, about 22 (about 24%) of the students (as opposed to 10, about 11%, in the pre-test) demonstrated an understanding that an electric current in a closed circuit moves in one direction around the circuit and that electric current will not be consumed (scientist's model, M3). The number of students who had the misconception that an electric current did not have to move round the whole circuit (unipolar model) dropped by 13% (23 of the students [about 25%] in the pre-test and 11 [about 12%] in the post-test). The number of students who still held the misconception that an electric current would be consumed as it moved round the circuit (current consumer model) decreased remarkably by 24% (50 of the students [about 55%] in the pre-test to 28 [about 31%] in the post-test).

Table 5.1 Metaphor(s) chosen and possible conceptions held by the students in the pre- and post-tests

Metaphor chosen and possible conception held by the students	Number of students	
	Pre-test	Post-test
M1: Clashing current model	8	18
M2: Current consumer model	50	28
M3: Scientist's model	10	22
M4: Unipolar model	23	11
Cannot be categorized / did not attempt	21	20

Note: Some students subscribed to more than one model. The numbers for M1, M2, and M4, include students who subscribed to more than one model. For M3, those choosing M3 only are included.

- On the question asking about the brightness of a light bulb at four positions in a circuit, 54 (about 59%) of the students in the post-test indicated that the brightness would be the same, and of these, 14 students gave explanations that conformed to the scientist's model. Whereas in the pre-test, only 32 (about 35%) of the students indicated that the brightness would be the same, only two students gave explanations that conform to the scientist's model.
- About 34% (31) more of the students indicated correctly that the bulb in the circuit with more cells was brighter on the post-test (67 of the students [about 74%] when compared to the pre-test (36 students, about 40%).

Conception shown in the students' explanations	Number of students	
	Pre-test	Post-test
The size of current is the SAME at the four positions		
S1: Scientist's model	2	14
S2: Unipolar model	0	3
No reason could be provided/no explanation provided	12	28
Cannot be categorized	18	9
Sub-total:	*32*	*54*
The size of current is DIFFERENT at the four positions		
D1: Current consumer model	4	10
D2: Unipolar model	0	3
No reason could be provided/no explanation provided	4	6
Cannot be categorized	7	6
Sub-total:	*15*	*25*
Irrelevant/did not attempt		
Sub-total:	*44*	*12*
Total:	*91*	*91*

The average scores on the four questions described above attained by the whole P4 level, and by those students who scored zero in the pre-test (referred to as the "lower achieving group"), in the pre- and post-test were compared. The marking scheme, the score distribution, and the results are shown in Tables 5.2, 5.3, and 5.4 respectively.

As shown in Table 5.3, both groups of students showed significant improvement on all test items, except the one requiring them to explain why they thought that the size of the current would be the same or different at the four positions of the circuit. This might be due to the fact that the students were weak at expressing themselves. Furthermore, Table 5.4 shows that, while the average score of the whole level improved by 1.20 out of a total of 5, the gain score of the lower achieving group was even greater: 1.84. It therefore provides evidence to support our belief that the lower achieving group can learn if the lesson is structured in ways to enable them to learn.

2.   Classroom observation

Classroom observation was another tool used for assessing the effect of the research lesson in the Learning Study. It was noted that the students were very interested and actively engaged in the group experiments. They were able to set up the circuit in many different ways to test whether the bulb would be lit. These included open and closed circuits. Some students also investigated some short circuits. The students' work contributed to the variations relevant for bringing about one of the critical features — electric current flows only in a closed circuit.

Table 5.2 The marking scheme

Question	Marking Scheme	
	Marking Item	Score
1. Choose from the given circuits the ones that would cause a bulb to light up	Correct Incorrect	1 0
2. Choose the most appropriate metaphor to describe the flow of an electric current in a closed circuit.	Scientist's model Other models or leave blank	1 0
3. Compare the size of the current at four positions in a circuit, and explain.	The same size Different or leave blank	1 0
	Explanation conforming to the scientist's model Explanation conforming to other models or leave blank	1 0
4. Compare the brightness of the light bulbs connected to two circuits, one with only one battery and the other two.	Correct Incorrect	1 0
	TOTAL SCORE:	5

Table 5.3 The score distribution of the two groups of students in the pre- and post-test

Question	Marking Item	Number of students (%)			
		Whole level (n=91)		Lower achieving group (n=38)	
		Pre-test	Post-test	Pre-test	Post-test
1	Correct	4 (4%)	54 (59%)	0 (0%)	22 (58%)
	Incorrect	87 (96%)	37 (41%)	38 (100%)	16 (42%)
2	Scientist's model	0 (0%)	22 (24%)	0 (0%)	11 (29%)
	Other models or leave blank	91 (100%)	69 (76%)	38 (100%)	27 (71%)
3	The same size	31 (34%)	54 (59%)	0 (0%)	25 (66%)
	Different or leave blank	60 (66%)	37 (41%)	38 (100%)	13 (34%)
	Explanation conforming to the scientist's model	2 (2%)	14 (15%)	0 (0%)	6 (16%)
	Explanation conforming to other models or leave blank	89 (98%)	77 (85%)	38 (100%)	32 (84%)
4	Correct	36 (40%)	67 (74%)	0 (0%)	27 (71%)
	Incorrect	55 (60%)	24 (26%)	38 (100%)	11 (29%)

Table 5.4 A comparison table of the average scores attained
by the two groups of students in the pre- and post-tests

	Total Score (total=5)	
	Whole level (n=91)	Lower achieving group (n=38)
Pre-test	0.62	0.00
Post-test	1.82	1.84
Change from pre-test to post-test	+1.20	+1.84

The students enjoyed the activities used to explain how an electric current flows in a circuit, using metaphors. They were able to point out what each part represented and the shortcomings of some of the metaphors.

Reflection on the research lesson

The teachers were delighted that most of their students (about 80%) could point out precisely what a closed circuit should look like. They also found it encouraging that the improvement in the students became greater (see Table 5.5) when they tried to modify the lesson plan to include more enriched variation to help the students focus on the difference between an open and a closed circuit (see Table 5.6).

More relevant variations were used in the second and third cycles. The results in the post-test also indicated a greater improvement in these cycles (88% and 85% respectively compared with 65% in the first cycle).

Although there was a significant drop (by 24%) in the number of students who had the misconception that an electric current will be consumed when moving round the circuit, the teachers were not satisfied with the result. One of the teachers pointed out that the use of metaphors may not be sufficient to help the students learn such an abstract concept, especially when they tried to avoid using terms like "atoms" and "electrons" in the discussion. Therefore, it was suggested that an experiment showing that the size of the electric current measured at different points of a closed circuit is the same could be added to give the students some concrete evidence. The teachers also felt that perhaps the notions of "atom" and "electron' could be used in explaining these metaphors and suggested that this might be tested out in the next cycle of research lessons on this topic.

It was also noticed that the number of students subscribing to the clashing current model increased from eight in the pre-test to 18 in the post-test (see Table 5.1). A possible explanation for such an increase is that the students had in general understood that an electric current could only flow in a complete circuit. This is also supported by the decrease in the number of students conforming to the unipolar model. However, some of them might still have difficulty in grasping that the current flows in one direction only.

Table 5.5 The students' performance in identifying the circuits that can light up a bulb in each of the three cycles on the post-test

	First cycle	Second cycle	Third cycle
No. of students who could identify the correct circuits (%)	17 (65%)	29 (88%)	28 (85%)

Table 5.6 Improvements made to the pattern of variation used in Part 2: Group experiment in setting up a circuit

	First cycle	Second cycle	Third cycle
Invariant	Components provided for setting up a circuit: a small 1.5 V light bulb, wires, a battery; or a lamp stand plugged into the power socket		
Variation	• Successful (closed circuits) and unsuccessful (open circuits) ways of setting up a circuit to light a bulb.		
		• Tracing out the path of the current in the successful circuits (closed paths) and comparing them with the unsuccessful circuits (paths not closed).	
		• Changing the unsuccessful ways of setting up a circuit into successful ones (from open to closed paths)	
	• A normal 60W bulb and a 60W bulb with the filament broken (closed vs. open path/circuit)		
		• Tracing out the path of the current in the normal bulb and the bulb with filament broken (closed vs. open circuit)	

This suggests that more effort has to be made in reinforcing the students' concept about the direction of the flow of electric current in a circuit.

The teachers also expressed in the individual teacher interviews conducted after this cycle of study that they found themselves experiencing a great leap forward, particularly regarding their knowledge in the subject:

> We would not have considered teaching in such great depth had we not participated in the research lessons. I did not even understand the content myself at the beginning. (CYY TI 0203)

> Actually, I had a lot of things that I did not know (about the topic of "electric current") because I majored in arts, not science. … but after several meetings, I began to understand what was critical to the learning of the topic ("electric current"). (WWY TI 0203)

Summing up

In this study, the teachers, in collaboration with the research team, tried to cater for individual differences by carefully examining their past experiences and the research literature, to identify possible difficulties or misconceptions that children of this age group usually have in learning the topic of "electricity" and to identify worthwhile objects of learning. Thus, instead of delivering the facts stated in the school textbook, they chose to focus mainly on the conceptual understanding of "closed circuit." Students' different ways of understanding about the flow of electric current in a closed circuit (V1) were then collected from the pre-test and analysed to identify the critical aspects/features which the students must grasp in order to overcome their difficulties in acquiring the objects of learning. Patterns of variation (V3) were then planned and implemented in the research lesson, to make possible the acquisition of the critical aspects/features. The lesson observation and the subsequent effort made to improve the lesson plan to enrich the pattern of variation in each cycle of the research lesson in this study are also important for addressing individual differences which may emerge only in the course of teaching. This can be shown by the fact that, when the pattern of variation was enhanced, the improvement in the students became greater (as aforementioned).

We were particularly delighted with the learning demonstrated by the teachers. We cannot hope to change a non-science teacher into a competent science teacher in a matter of months; however, through this Learning Study, we have demonstrated that even a non-science teacher can be helped to teach competently a science lesson with confidence and can facilitate deep learning of the students in science.

Furthermore, the teachers and researchers, in the course of developing such teaching, found themselves being rewarded by the significant improvement in the students, specifically that the average gain score attained by those who scored zero in the pre-test was even greater than the average. This gave us more confidence and faith in our approach to catering for individual differences through Learning Study. Also, the students' difficulties in learning this topic that were found to be persistent in the post-test provide the team with valuable resources for the next cycle of research lessons in improving the teaching and learning of "electric current."

Primary 4 General Studies: Price

(PANG Ming Fai and Pakey CHIK Pui Man)

The Learning Study group comprised five P4 general studies teachers and three research team members. The entire cycle of the study lasted from 11

October 2002 to 29 May 2003, during which 11 meetings (including five post-lesson conferences) were held in the school during after-school hours. The development of the study included four stages: incubation of ideas, lesson planning, teaching of the research lesson, and evaluation of the research lesson.

Stage I: Incubation of ideas

Choosing the topic

In the first meeting, the group tried to identify a topic for the study that would engender deep and meaningful learning in students while matching the progress of the syllabus. To achieve the aims of general studies to provide "learning experiences for students to have a better understanding of themselves and the world around them" (CDC 2002), the group decided to focus the research lesson on the topic of "price." This is conceived to be part of the school-based curriculum of the school involved, which follows the principles of curriculum management to "identify entry points for school-based curriculum development" (CDC 2002).

This topic was chosen for the following two reasons. Firstly, it was considered worthwhile for the students to learn, because it is one of the most fundamental concepts in economics. A good understanding of this abstract concept can help students develop a better understanding of the world around them, especially the Hong Kong economy. Secondly, the teachers believed that the learning of this topic would lay a good foundation for students studying the topic "where to shop" in the P4 general studies syllabus, and in the long run for their learning in the key learning area of personal, social and humanities education at secondary level, which is highlighted in the official curriculum document (CDC 2002).

Identifying the object of learning

Having decided on the topic, the group started to discuss what students might find difficult to learn about "price." Reference was made to related research papers (e.g., Dahlgren 1978, 1979; Thomas 1983, 1985; Pong 2000), from which it was found that small children tended to think that the price of a good is determined by its properties (e.g., size), whereas the higher-grade students would consider the demand of the good the major determinant of its price. Only a few students were aware of the importance of the demand-supply interaction on the price of a good, which is a more comprehensive consideration of "price."

A teacher also pointed out that, in a "selling and buying" activity she introduced to a P3 mathematics lesson about money exchange, the students were inclined to mark up the price when selling goods and to lower the price when buying goods. This then reflects that the students' ways of seeing "price" were incomplete, which is consistent with what was found in the research papers.

Therefore, the research lesson was aimed at enriching students' ways of understanding "price," the critical aspect being the effect of both demand and supply factors on "price."

Designing a pre-test

A pre-test was then set, aiming to collect more information about the students' understanding of "price." After a lively discussion, the group decided to set a question in the context of selling hotdogs in the school's tuck-shop. Since hot dogs were actually a popular item in the tuck-shop, it would be very interesting and easy for the students to express their ideas. The question was finalized as follows:

> Have you ever tried the hot dogs sold in our school tuck-shop? Do you know how much they cost? Maybe you know or you don't know. Anyway, just for your information, hot dogs are now sold at HK$4.50.
>
> Suppose that you were the new owner of the tuck-shop. What price would you set for a hot dog? Would you set the current price, or a different price? What would you consider when you set the price?

The pre-test was administered to 176 P4 students. The result is summarized in the table below:

Conception of "price" reflected in the answer	No. of students	Percentage
A. Supply and demand (e.g., the number of sellers in the market and the purchasing power of the consumers)	12	6.8%
B. Supply (e.g., costs of production)	13	7.4%
C. Demand (e.g., number of people who buy hot dog)	99	56.2%
D. Nature of the good (e.g., condiment or size of hot dog)	13	7.4%
E. Unclassified (e.g., the hot dog should be sold at $1)	32	18.2%
F. Other reasons (e.g., students' academic performance)	7	4%
Total:	176	100%

In general, the pre-test results showed that most students regarded "demand" as the main factor affecting their decision on setting the price of a hotdog. Few of them considered the supply factors, and few took both supply and demand factors into consideration. This is consistent with the research findings that show that students do not have a comprehensive way of seeing "price." The group continued with the design of the lesson, focusing on bringing out the identified critical aspect of seeing price in a comprehensive way, i.e., the importance of both the demand and supply of the commodity on "price."

Stage II: Lesson Planning

In the development of the lesson plan, the teachers decided to use a double period, focusing on sensitizing students to the importance of both demand and supply factors on "price." To help students to learn, the context of "holding an auction to raise funds for the school's current construction project" was used. In this context, various scenarios were created. The teacher purposefully varied either demand or supply factors of certain goods while keeping the demand and supply factors of the others invariant. In doing so, students were allowed to think of how to determine the price in a given situation. The detailed teaching flow and the use of variation are as follows:

Lesson plan (80 minutes)

A. Introduction: (three to five minutes)
1. Teacher introduces the idea of an auction to raise funds for the school's current construction project.
2. Teacher explains the procedures and regulations of the auction:
    Teacher will be the auctioneer and students will form groups to bid for the items under the auction.
        There will be four auctioned items: mechanical dinosaur, doll, dinosaur card, and stationery set. The samples of each item are displayed on the teacher's desk.
        Before the auction, each group of students should nominate a representative to bid for the items. In the course of bidding, the representatives have to raise the given auction sign.

B. Development

Scenario I (15 minutes):

1. Teaching flow
(a) Teacher shows the quantity, the price, and the bid of each of the auctioned items, using the auction recording table on the blackboard:

Auction Recording Table:

	Mechanical dinosaur	Doll	Dinosaur card	Stationery set
Quantity	2	2	3	3
Floor price	80	60	20	20
Amount for each bid	20	20	10	10
Auctioned price				

(b) Teacher assigns the auction money of $200 or $300 to the groups randomly, and states: You must try your best to bid for at least one item in order to win the game.

(c) Before the auction begins, students need to note down their individual decision and the group's finalized decision on the following questions on Worksheets (1) and (2) respectively:
  • What do you want to bid for?
  • How much are you willing to bid for them?
  • What are the prices paid for the items?

(d) Auction begins. Teacher records the auctioned price for each item in the auction recording table. The items bought by each group and the money they have left are also recorded on the blackboard in the auctioning process.

(e) Auction ends. Students are instructed to write down the prices paid for the items on the worksheets.

(f) Teacher discusses with students the following questions:
  • Are the prices paid at the auction reasonable? Why?
  • Are the prices paid the same as the amount that you are willing to bid for the items? Why?

2. Use of variation:
   2.1 This scenario is set up to contrast with the next two scenarios.

Scenario II:

1. Teaching flow
(a) Expecting that some students will account for the results in Scenario I by saying that the auctioned prices increase when compared with the floor prices due to the fact that competition is keen, the teacher introduces Scenario II: Is it true that prices will go up when the competition becomes very keen? Let us investigate this situation by reducing the supply of each of the items now.

(b) Teacher revises the quantity of each item in the auction recording table accordingly:

Auction Recording Table

	Mechanical dinosaur	Doll	Dinosaur card	Stationery set
Quantity	changed from 2 to 1	changed from 2 to 1	changed from 3 to 2	changed from 3 to 2
Floor price	80	60	20	20
Amount for each bid	20	20	10	10
Auctioned price				

(c) Teacher randomly re-assigns the auction money ($200 or $300) to the groups, to avoid disputes, and repeats: You must try your best to bid for at least one item in order to win the game.

(d) Before the auction begins, students need to note down their individual decision and the group's finalized decision on the following questions on Worksheets (1) and (2) respectively:
   • What do you want to bid for?
   • How much are you willing to bid for them?
   • What are the prices paid for the items?

(e) Auction begins. Teacher records the auctioned price for each item in the auction recording table. The items bought by each group and the money they have left are also recorded on the blackboard in the auctioning process.

(f) Auction ends. Students are instructed to write down the prices paid for the items on the worksheets.

(g) Teacher discusses with students the following questions:
   • Are the prices paid at the auction reasonable? Why?
   • Are the prices paid the same as the maximum amount that you are willing to bid for the items? Why?
   • What happened to the prices paid when compared with those in the last auction (Scenario I)? Can you explain this?

(h) Teacher points out that the situation has changed. In this auction, we had a lower supply of the items, and you had to compete for the more limited supply. The teacher then states that, given that the purchasing power (and thus the demand for the goods) remains unchanged, the lower the supply, the higher the market price.

2. Use of variation:
(a) In this scenario, the teacher purposely introduces variation in the supply by reducing the number of each item available while keeping the auction money (purchasing power: one of the demand factors) unchanged. It is hoped that, by doing so, the students' focus would be on the relationship between a change in supply and the resulting market "price," i.e., given the demand, when supply decreases, the price will go up, and vice versa.

Invariant	Variation	Critical aspect to be discerned
The demand for the goods (by keeping the auction money or the purchasing power unchanged), the nature of the goods	The supply of the goods; the auctioned prices	The relationship between the supply of the goods and their prices

Scenario III:

1. Teaching flow
(a) Teacher introduces Scenario III: Imagine that we have a serious economic recession now. So, everyone earns less and your auction money will thus be reduced by $100. What will happen to the prices paid at the auction if the original quantities of the items are up for bidding again?

   In economics, demand is defined as the amount of goods that people are both *willing and able* to buy at all prices. It is a planned schedule in people's mind only. The factors affecting demand for a good may include taste (which will affect people's willingness to buy), income (which will affect people's ability to buy), etc. Given that the goods are normal goods, the less income people have, the lower their demand for the goods will be. So, in this lesson we deliberately reduced the auction money of each group so that they would have less income to spend. We presumed that their taste or willingness to buy would not drastically change within such a short time; their demand for the goods would then decrease accordingly.
(b) Teacher resumes the quantity of each of the auctioned items in the auction recording table as in Scenario I, in order to enable students to understand the effect of a change in auction money on the prices of the goods:

Auction Recording Table:

	Mechanical dinosaur	Doll	Dinosaur card	Stationery set
Quantity	2	2	3	3
Floor price	80	60	20	20
Amount for each bid				
Auctioned price	20	20	10	10

(c) Teacher randomly re-assigns the auction money ($100 or $200) to the groups, to avoid disputes, and repeats: You must try your best to bid for at least one item in order to win the game.
(d) Before the auction begins, students need to note down their individual decision and the group's finalized decision on the following questions on Worksheets (1) and (2) respectively:

- What do you want to bid for?
- How much are you willing to bid for them?
- What are the prices paid for the items?

(e) Auction begins. Teacher records the price paid for each item in the auction recording table. The items bought by each group and the money they have left are also recorded on the blackboard in the auctioning process.

(f) Auction ends. Students are instructed to write down the prices paid for the items on the worksheets.

(g) Teacher discusses with students the following questions:
- Are the prices paid at the auction reasonable? Why?
- Are the prices paid the same as the maximum amount that you are willing to bid for the items? Can you explain this situation?
- What happened to the prices paid when compared with those resulting in Scenario I? Can you explain this?

(h) Teacher concludes from the discussion: Since you were given less money this time, you were not able to offer a higher price for the auctioned goods. So, the prices paid at the auction were lower than those in the first auction.

2. Use of variation:

(a) In this scenario, the teacher purposely introduces a variation in the demand, by cutting down the groups' auction money (i.e., their purchasing power) while keeping the quantities of the auctioned items (the supply) unchanged. It is hoped that, by doing so, students will focus on the effect of the change in demand on "price," i.e., given the supply, when demand decreases, the price will go down, and vice versa.

Invariant	Variation	Critical aspect to be discerned
The supply of the goods, the nature of the goods	The demand for the goods (by cutting down auction money or the purchasing power); the auctioned prices	The relationship between the demand of the goods and their prices

C. Conclusion and Consolidation (15 to 20 minutes)

1. Teaching flow

(a) Teacher introduces Worksheet (3), the content of which is translated as follows:

Suppose you are the owner of a stationery shop, and the price of a mechanical dinosaur was $80 two weeks ago. Now, there are only a few machines available in the market, and people are earning more money as the economy is growing. Will you change the price of the mechanical dinosaur? Why?

(b) Students complete the worksheet individually.

(c) After students have completed the worksheet, teacher discusses with students their answers and helps them to arrive at the conclusion: The price of a commodity is actually determined by both market demand and supply.

2. Use of variation:

(a) In the question, both the demand and supply varied simultaneously, and students were to determine the price of a commodity (i.e., mechanical dinosaur) by taking into account the simultaneous variation in both the economic conditions (i.e., the variation in the income of people as a result of the change in the economic condition) as well as the number of goods available (e.g., the supply of the original mechanical dinosaur) embedded in the question.

Invariant	Variation	Critical aspect to be discerned
The nature of the goods	The demand of and supply for the goods; The auctioned prices	The interaction of demand and supply in determining the price of the goods

Trying out the lesson plan

A trial teaching session was arranged before the actual research lesson, aimed at familiarizing the teachers with the teaching flow and making suitable amendments. The trial lesson ran smoothly. Some amendments were made to the lesson plan. These are summarized as follows:

• Have students sit in groups before the lesson begins, to save time for the teaching.

• Cancel the differentiation in auction money assigned to different groups of students, to avoid unnecessary complications.

• Tell students that there will be a fixed quantity for each auctioned item. Each item will be open for bidding only once. The highest bidder will get one, whereas other bidders who are willing and able to offer the auctioned price will get the others. If no one is willing and able to offer the same price, the remaining item(s) will be taken off the auction list.

• Instead of having students complete one worksheet individually and another in groups, only use the worksheet for group discussions, to avoid confusion and to save time for the auction and the subsequent discussion.

• Prepare sentence strips for the conclusions made in Scenario II and III. Stick them on the blackboard after the auction and the subsequent discussions in the two scenarios respectively, for consolidation purposes.

Phrase the conclusions in such a way that students' attention can be drawn to the point that the change in prices results from either a change in supply or demand in different scenarios:

Scenario II: *Given that purchasing power (auction money) remains unchanged, when the supply decreases, the price increases.*

Scenario III: *Given that the supply remains unchanged, when the purchasing power (auction money) decreases, the price decreases.*

- Use a "scale" chart (see Figure 5.4 below) to show the interaction between supply and demand in determining the price.
- Discuss with the students the question stated in the consolidation worksheet that involves a simultaneous variation in both supply and demand, before completing the worksheet.
- Make full use of the blackboard to display the various teaching aids, by dividing it into three columns: one for the money balance sheet, one for the auction recording table, and one for the conclusion sentence strips and the "scale" chart.

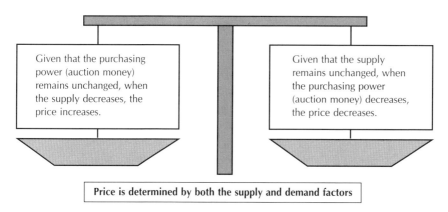

Given that the purchasing power (auction money) remains unchanged, when the supply decreases, the price increases.

Given that the supply remains unchanged, when the purchasing power (auction money) decreases, the price decreases.

Price is determined by both the supply and demand factors

Figure 5.4 The "scale" chart

Stage III: Teaching in the Research Lesson

Five teachers taught the research lesson to their classes (Classes A to E) in the period 6 to 19 March 2003, in five cycles. In each cycle, two teachers teamed up in teaching while other members of the group observed. A post-lesson conference immediately followed. In the conference, the teachers shared the insights and observations made during the lessons. All five lessons were videotaped for the purpose of evaluation and for further studies. Major changes made to smooth the flow of teaching after each cycle are detailed as follows.

After the first cycle

- **The auction:**
  a. Reverse the order of Scenario II (supply reduced) and Scenario III (purchasing power decreased), to attain better contrasts with Scenario I.
  b. Devote more time for students' discussion (especially if they have contrasting opinions).

- **Conclusion and consolidation:**
  Change the context of the question (see below) so that students could focus on the simultaneous change in both the supply and demand factors instead of being distracted by something else, such as "The machines are left over, and people may not want them even if they have money," as suggested by a student in the lesson.
  "*As you know, the mechanical dinosaur is now selling at $80 in the toyshops. Suppose that you are the owner of a large toyshop, which is the sole supplier of the new model. It has not been publicly released and is issued as a limited version. At the same time, you observe that the Hong Kong economy has been recovering very well over this period. Given these conditions, what price will you set for this new model? Why?*"

After the second cycle

- **The auction**:
  Distribute a strip of paper with a short conclusion printed on it after each of the auctions in Scenario II and Scenario III has finished, to help draw students' attention from the bidding activity to discussing what the results of each auction tell us about the notion of "market price."

After the third cycle

- **The auction**:
  a. Illustrate the term "purchasing power" with examples familiar to students (e.g., their pocket money), to facilitate their understanding of the scenarios and the conclusions drawn.
  b. It was observed that, in the second cycle, when the students' purchasing power was decreased (by cutting their pocket money), they were less willing to bid for goods (especially those with a higher floor price in Scenario II). The reason was that they wished to keep their purchasing power for buying goods at a lower floor price. However, because the order in which the goods appeared was such that some of those with higher floor prices came first, when students gave up

their chance to buy these goods, many of them had to compete for buying those with a lower floor price when these appeared later. This resulted in higher auctioned prices for the goods with a lower floor price, thus making it difficult to draw the conclusion that, "given that supply remains unchanged, when the purchasing power (auction money) decreases, the price decreases." Therefore, it was suggested that the order in which the goods appeared for bidding in each scenario (see the table below) be changed, instead of going about it randomly as in the previous cycles. It was hoped by this modification that the resulting auctioned prices could be better controlled for comparison purposes.

Auction	Good 1	Good 2	Good 3	Good 4
First round	Lower floor price	Higher floor price	Higher floor price	Lower floor price
Second round (less demand)	Lower floor price	Lower floor price	Higher floor price	Higher floor price
Third round (less supply)	Higher floor price	Higher floor price	Lower floor price	Lower floor price

After the fourth cycle

- **Conclusion and consolidation:**
  Leave more time for students' discussion, and build up the "scale" chart accordingly as a wrap-up of the lesson.

Stage IV: Evaluating the Effects of the Research Lesson

The learning outcomes

1. Comparison between the pre- and post-test results

   A post-test, which is parallel to the pre-test, was administered to the students after each cycle of the research lesson had been completed. All the students who attended both the pre- and post-tests were included in the analysis. The students' conceptions of "price" as reflected in their answers on the pre- and post-tests were categorized and are compared in Table 5.7. The breakdown for each class is shown in Table 5.8.

   As shown in Table 5.7, there was about a 20% increase in the percentage of students whose answers were classified in the category of "supply and demand," demonstrating a comprehensive concept of "price" (from 6.3% in the pre-test to 26.4% in the post-test).

Table 5.7 Comparison of the students' conceptions of "price"
as reflected in their answers on the pre- and post-tests

Conception of "price" reflected in the answer	Pre-test		Post-test	
	No. of students	Percentage	*No. of students*	Percentage
A. Supply and demand	11	6.8%	42	25.9%
B. Supply	11	6.8%	9	5.6%
C. Demand	92	56.8%	85	52.5%
D. Nature of the good	12	7.4%	11	6.8%
E. Unclassified	30	18.5%	14	8.6%
F. Other reasons	6	3.7%	1	0.6%
Total	162	100%	162	100%

Table 5.8 The breakdown of the students' conceptions of "price" for each class

Conception of "price" reflected in the answer	4A (high ability)		4B (high ability)		4C (average ability)	
	Pre-test	Post-test	Pre-test	Post-test	Pre-test	Post-test
A. Supply and demand	3.0%	9.1%	10.3%	61.5%	3.2%	12.9%
B. Supply	0.0%	6.0%	2.6%	7.7%	3.2%	3.2%
C. Demand	39.4%	45.5%	64.0%	28.2%	77.5%	71.0%
D. Nature of the good	6.1%	15.2%	7.7%	0.0%	0.0%	9.7%
E. Unclassified	48.5%	24.2%	7.7%	0.0%	16.1%	3.2%
F. Other reasons	3.0%	0.0%	7.7%	2.6%	0.0%	0.0%

Conception of "price" reflected in the answer	4D (low ability)		4E (average ability)	
	Pre-test	Post-test	Pre-test	Post-test
A. Supply and demand	7.1%	14.2%	9.7%	22.6%
B. Supply	10.7%	3.6%	19.4%	6.5%
C. Demand	50.0%	78.6%	51.5%	48.4%
D. Nature of the good	17.9%	0.0%	6.5%	9.7%
E. Unclassified	10.7%	3.6%	9.7%	12.8%
F. Other reasons	3.6%	0.0%	3.2%	0.0%

Table 5.8 also shows that, although there were gains in all classes in the percentage of students who demonstrated a comprehensive concept of "price," the highest and the lowest gains were noted in the two perceived high-ability classes, Class 4B (about 51.2% increase) and Class 4A (about 6.1% increase) respectively. This supports our claim that some children fail to learn not because of their innate ability but because they are not provided with learning

experiences that enable them to learn. It was therefore important for us to investigate what actually happened in Class 4B that contributed to the exceptional performance of the students when compared with other classes.

According to the lesson plan, after the first round of auctioning, the intention was to have a scenario in which there was no change in supply but a decrease in purchasing power (i.e., the demand factor) when compared with the first round. The introduction of this scenario aimed at showing the effect of the demand factor on determining the price of a good, i.e., "given the same supply of a good, the price will go down when there is a decrease in purchasing power (i.e., the demand factor)." However, in Class 4B, the auctioned price of one of the items ($190) in such a scenario was higher than the price of the same auctioned item obtained in the first round ($110). The teacher was aware that this turned out to be deflected from their original intention of focusing the students' attention on the effect of the demand factor on deciding price. Thus, he immediately offered two more of the same item for auctioning, and a group of students succeeded in buying it at the floor price ($20) when no other group seemed to be interested in bidding for it. The following is an excerpt of the whole class discussion on why two different prices resulted for the auctioning of the very same item.

T:	Group 2, tell us why you were willing to pay such a high price ($190) for the dinosaur card (one of the auctioned items)?
Ss in Group 2:	Because we thought that there would be only one auction for it (the dinosaur card). By that time, we didn't know that it would be offered for the second time and were afraid of getting none of the items.
T:	So, this is why you were willing to pay such a high price. ... (Turning to ask other groups of students). But when I offered two more dinosaur cards for auctioning, why didn't you try to bid for them, except Group 5?
S1:	Because we had used up our money already.
S2:	Well, we had successfully bid for one of the items already. We didn't need *more*.

In this way, although the activity failed to achieve its original purpose, it allowed simultaneous variation in both the demand factor (a decrease in purchasing power when compared with the first round) and the supply factor (an increase of the quantity of the same item offered for auctioning in the scenario) to come into play. This had the result of bringing the students' attention to the effect of the demand-supply interaction on the price of a good. Such a simultaneous variation was, however, absent from other classes, in which no additional auction had been introduced with any of the auctioned goods. Thus we see that students in Class 4B showed a better grasp of the demand-supply interaction determining the price of a good.

Table 5.7 shows that, in general, a majority of the students were still inclined to look for the demand factors on deciding "price" in the post-test. In particular, the percentage of students whose answers fell into the category "demand" increased in Class 4A (by 6.1%) and Class 4D (by 28.6%) in the post-test (see Table 5.8). When looking closely into the teaching enactment, a similar discussion was observed in the two classes on why the auctioned prices obtained in Scenario III, when there was no change in purchasing power but a decrease in supply when compared with Scenario I, were higher than the prices obtained in Scenario I:

> T: Look at the auctioned prices obtained in this round and the first round of auctioning. What is different?
> S1: The auctioned prices obtained in this round are much higher than those in the first round.
> T: Yes. The auctioned prices we had in this round are much higher. Can you tell why?
> S2: Because most of us didn't want to lose in this round, so we competed strongly with one another and spent as much money as possible to bid for the goods.
> T: So, you didn't want to lose. That is why you were willing to pay high prices for the goods... Okay, let's not look at other factors. Just look at the quantity of each auctioned item offered in the two rounds and the resulting auctioned *prices*. What do you find?
> S3: I know. The quantity of each of the auctioned items in this round is lower than that in the first round, and so the auctioned prices we had in this round are higher than those in the first round.
> T: Right...
> S4: (interrupting what the teacher was going to say) That means we had stronger competition in this round because we didn't want to lose.

Thus, a demand factor (i.e., students' desire to bid for the goods in order to win) other than the predetermined one (i.e., purchasing power) emerged in the discussion. Unfortunately, the teacher missed the opportunity to help students to link their anxiety of not being able to buy any goods to the decreasing supply of the goods. Thus, instead of focusing on the change in supply, the emphasis was put on the variation in students' desire to bid for the goods. This kind of discussion drawing students' attention to the demand factor happened only in Classes 4A and 4D. Also, in Class 4D, some of the students suggested that the higher auctioned prices in Scenario III were a result of the increase in their purchasing power ($300) when compared with that in Scenario II ($150). Thus, a dimension of variation in purchasing power was also opened up, again drawing the students' attention to the effect of the demand factor on determining the prices of the goods. Table 5.9 (see p. 111) compares the pattern of variation constituted in different classes.

Table 5.9 Comparison of the pattern of variation constituted in Scenario III different classes

	4B, C, E	4A	4D
Invariant	• Purchasing power (the given auction money)		
Variation	• The supply of the auctioned goods in Scenario III increased when compared with that in Scenario I.		
	• The auctioned prices in Scenario III increased when compared with those in Scenario I.		
		• Stronger desire to win in Scenario III when compared with Scenario I.	
			• The purchasing power increased in Scenario III when compared with Scenario II.

Individual students' answers in the pre- and post-tests were also analysed to trace their change of conception of "price." The results are summarized as follows:

- About 37% of the students showed improvement (e.g., answers categorized as "nature of the good" in the pre-test and "supply and demand" in the post-test).
- About 40.3% of the students did not have a change in the conception of price (e.g., answers categorized as "supply" in both pre- and post-test, or in the same level: "supply" in the pre-test and "demand" in the post-test).
- About 12.2% of the students dropped in performance (e.g., answers categorized as "demand" in the pre-test and "nature of the good" in the post-test).
- About 10.5% of the students' answers could not be classified.

Overall, given that the concept is very advanced and abstract for students at Primary 4 level, and only one double lesson was spent on this, the results are encouraging. About 40% of the students showed improvement in their conception of "price" after the research lesson. It suggests that the research lesson had a positive effect on students' learning.

2. Student interviews

Besides using the pre- and post-test data, the research team also collected data from student interviews which were arranged after each research lesson. There were usually five to six students participating in each interview. The research team would ask them questions, like the following:
- Was the lesson interesting?
- What have you learnt in the lesson?
- Do you know how to determine price?

Some scenarios were also suggested to probe students' understanding. Examples are: "Suppose the economy is bad at present, and there is a large quantity of a certain commodity in the market. What do you think will happen to the price?" "What do you think about the price of a flat? Does the price rise or fall? Why?"

Using face-to-face conversation, the students were able to express and explain their ideas on "price" directly. In general, students' performances in the interviews were encouraging, and many of them demonstrated a good understanding of the concept of how to determine price, by taking into account both the demand- and supply-side factors. Though most of the answers were not sophisticated, it appeared that, for Primary 4 students, it was an advancement in their economic understanding of the notion of market price.

Reflective comments

1. The research lesson
    *   In the early research meetings, the teachers were worried that the topic of "price" might be too difficult for Primary 4 students. However, having taught the lesson and observed each other's teaching, they were pleased to find that the students actually learnt quite well how "price" is determined in the market.
    *   Since the students were provided with many opportunities to express their ideas on "price" in the research lesson, the teachers found that they could better understand how their students experienced the phenomenon of price. Furthermore, the students were found to be very active in expressing their views. They also learnt to appreciate others' opinions, and to compromise when viewpoints differed.
    *   The teachers believed that this research lesson served as a very good starting point in preparing the students for the long-term development of economic literacy. Therefore, they planned to continue the study with the same group of students in Primary 5 in the next academic year.

2. The use of the Theory of Variation
    *   Some teachers reflected that they became conscious of using variation to design their lesson, which they might have used but were seldom aware of before joining the project. In teaching, they purposely varied certain aspect(s) (e.g., the demand factor) while keeping the others invariant, so that the students could focus on how the varying aspect(s) affects the "price."
    *   A teacher who conducted the research lessons in another subject indicated that the outcomes of the conscious use of variation in teaching different subjects were encouraging, and she hoped that she could continue using it in other topics in the near future.

3. The Learning Study

    •   The teachers pointed out that Learning Study did provide them with a systematic way to plan, refine, and improve their teaching. In particular, in this Learning Study, the lesson plan was reviewed after each cycle of the research lesson. The review focused on students' difficulties as observed in the lesson, and changes were made to modify the plan, to avoid problems encountered in the lesson. As a result, the teachers found that the lesson plan was well thought-out and better able to cater for different classes in due course.

    •   They realized that not only do students have individual differences but so do teachers, and both are valuable resources for lesson planning.

    •   The teachers were also glad to have an opportunity to observe, share, and comment on each other's lessons in the study. The teachers expressed the view that the kind of cooperation and mutual support among the group through collaborative planning of the lesson, team-teaching the research lesson, and immediate post-lesson evaluation, not only represented a source of motivation but was also a catalyst for their own professional development.

    •   Through the close cooperation with the teachers, the researcher explored more teaching methods in dealing with primary students regarding "price." This experience has been valuable and will enhance his teaching and research in the future.

Summing up

Overall, the Learning Study, which is premised on the three types of variation — variation in students' ways of experiencing "price," variation in teachers' ways of experiencing the object of learning, and the use of variation as a guiding principle of pedagogical design to enhance students' learning — is found to be an effective tool to cater for individual differences. We aimed at actualizing the potential of every student by helping each one to learn what is worthwhile for him or her to learn in an effective and efficient way. As supported by the findings of this Learning Study, the pedagogy based on variation and discernment seemed to work well to bring about student learning. The teachers consciously made available a particular pattern of variation that led to a desired way of experiencing in the classrooms, and thus created a space of learning that enabled students to learn better, i.e., more students were empowered to see the phenomenon of "price" in a more comprehensive and sophisticated way.

However, the study has the following limitations. First of all, the team did not have sufficient time to take follow-up action to clarify with the students who had produced "unclassified" answers after the research lesson. We therefore had difficulty trying to recognize these students' ways of understanding that led to their conceptions. It is hoped that, in the next Learning Study cycle, follow-up work will be done to investigate such unclassified student answers so that we can provide some more tailor-made support for the students. Furthermore, the teachers believed that a double lesson might not be sufficient to finish the tasks set. It was recommended to arrange more lessons for the study so that students will be given ample time and opportunities to discuss and express their views. Nonetheless, we are not satisfied with the resulting student learning outcomes, although we restate that the object of learning is quite advanced for this level of students. A substantial portion of the students still held the conception of price that is determined by demand or supply alone. In the next cycle, more attention should be paid to helping students discern that either supply or demand alone will not determine the price of a commodity.

Summary

In this chapter, we illustrated with two studies how groups of teachers, in collaboration with the research team, carried out their Learning Studies in an attempt to enhance learning in students of different abilities. There are a number of insights into Learning Study as a tool to address the issue of catering for individual differences that can be drawn from these studies:

- Identifying worthwhile objects of learning for all students is not an easy task. Very often, the teachers would judge on their past experience what seemed to be the most difficult areas for their students and what constitute the critical aspects for students' further pursuit in learning, such as the study on "electricity." In some cases, the objects of learning were chosen because they served to enrich students' ways of seeing or understanding, like the study on "price."
- Exhausting students' different ways of understanding to refine the chosen objects of learning and to locate what was most critical for learning is another important yet difficult task in addressing the issue of catering for students' differences in learning. In some cases, the differences in students' understanding were more readily obtainable through the use of pre-test and from the literature, such as the concepts of "price." In other cases, such as "electricity," some critical features were only revealed during the research lesson and it would, sometimes, take cycles of study to find out all possible differences in students' understanding. This is why lesson observations and subsequent modifications made to the lesson plan between cycles of lesson are so important.

- Being sensitized to how students experience learning and to what constitute students' difficulties in learning, the teachers were in a better position to help their students learn more efficiently. Being able to share in the group was another contributing factor. As suggested by two of the general studies teachers in the study of "electricity," they were able to study in depth what to teach in the preparation meetings and became more confident in teaching the research lesson.

Some readers may wonder about the long-term effect of the research lesson, and why, in some cases, the improvement in scores was quite modest. In fact, each of the Learning Studies was focused on a research lesson that was also a part of the curriculum in the school. There are always lessons before it and lessons after it. What we have reported here is thus only a snapshot of the students' learning within a theme or a topic. It is normal for teachers to give students exercises for consolidation, and later lessons will revise and build on what has been previously learnt. Thus, the post-tests, which were usually carried out immediately after the research lessons, measured the effect of the teaching of the research lesson only. The reader therefore should not be misled into thinking that a research lesson is the only occasion for learning a particular object of learning; rather, it represents a part of the learning as a whole.

What is more, as we mentioned earlier in this chapter, research lessons are not model lessons. There is always room for improvement. Each Learning Study, however, helps us to understand more about how our students learn and how we as teachers or teacher educators can help them to learn more efficiently. The research lesson is not an end in itself. It should contribute to the next cycle of Learning Study on the same object of learning or topic. We hope that the readers can also take these factors as the basis for their first cycle of research lesson in their own schools.

6

The Effect of Learning Studies on Student Learning Outcomes

KWOK Wing Yin and Pakey CHIK Pui Man

In Chapter 4, we illustrated with evidence from the three-year research project how Learning Study can help to enhance the quality of teaching and learning through developing teachers' professionalism in improving the curriculum, pedagogy, and use of diagnostic assessment. We also described the development of learning studies in the two primary schools during the three years of the implementation of the research project (2000–03) and the rapid spread of the use of Learning Study to over 100 schools in both primary and secondary sectors in the subsequent academic year (2003–04). Such a wide acceptance and adoption of Learning Study in the community within a short period of no more than five years is indeed encouraging. However, we have to be careful in drawing any conclusion that Learning Study is therefore an effective way to cater for individual differences. In Chapter 5, two Learning Studies are provided to give an in-depth account of how teachers focus on a specific object of learning and work in a typical Learning Study cycle to produce a research lesson, and how teaching can be related to learning and be enhanced. In this chapter, we attempt to provide a more comprehensive picture of how well students of different abilities performed in the Learning Studies.

As explained in the previous chapters, the foremost step in a Learning Study is to identify the "object of learning" and the critical aspects/features associated with the object of learning. The pre-tests and post-tests are a major means to verify teachers' thinking in those regards. As such, the data from the pre-tests constitute an input to the planning of the research lesson by informing the team about students' prior understanding of the subject matter. The post-test, which is parallel to the pre-test, then shows the progress that the students have made with regard to the intended learning outcomes, and thus forms a basis for evaluating the effectiveness of the research lesson. Therefore, in this chapter, we describe the overall result of the data comparing students' gain scores between the pre-test and post-test in each of the learning studies conducted within the project. Triangulation is also made with the data of the Hong Kong Attainment Tests in mathematics and Chinese language for two groups of students who participated in the research lessons in either subject throughout the three years of the implementation.

Comparisons of students' gain scores on the pre-test and post-test

During the three academic years (2000/2001, 2001/2002, 2002/2003), a total of 29 Learning Studies were conducted. In 27 out of the 29 studies, pre-tests and post-tests were administered to the whole group of students who had participated in the research lessons, for diagnostic assessment. The other two studies, in which diagnostic tests were not administered to the whole group of students, were excluded from the analysis. The analysis consists of three types of comparison. The results are described in the following sections.

Comparisons between the mean scores of the whole group in the pre-test and post-test

In each of the twenty-seven studies, comparison was made between the mean scores in the pre-test and post-test of students who had attended the tests and the research lesson, and whose identities (e.g., name, class and class number) could be traced. A paired t-test (one-tailed) at the significance level of 0.05 (i.e., 95% significance) was also performed to examine if the change in mean score was significant, a null hypothesis being "the mean score of the whole group in the post-test is equal to or smaller than ($\leqq$) that in the pre-test." In other words, the refutation of the null hypothesis means that the mean score of the whole group in the post-test is significantly greater than that in the pre-test, i.e., the improvement students made in the post-test is significant on average. The results are summarized as follows (see also Table 6.1):

a. In all twenty-seven Learning Studies, there was an increase in the mean score of the whole group in the post-test.

b. In 24 out of the 27 studies, the increases in mean score in the post-test were significant on a paired t-test (one-tailed) at the significance level of 0.05. In particular, improvements that were statistically significant were noted in all of the six studies carried out in the third year of study (2002/03).

Comparisons between the mean scores of each score group in the pre-test and post-test

In each study, the mean scores attained by students at different levels of achievement in the pre-test and post-test were compared, to further examine

Table 6.1 A summary of the analysis for significant improvement in the mean score of the whole group in the post-test in each of the 27 Learning Studies carried out during the three academic years

Academic Year	No. of Learning Studies conducted	No. of studies in which the mean score increased in the post-test	No. of studies in which the increase in the mean score was significant
2000/01	6	6	5
2001/02	15	15	13
2002/03	6	6	6
Total	27	27	24

(Please refer to Appendix 4 for more detailed information and result of the analysis for each study.)

whether students of different abilities could benefit from the research lesson. For the purpose of comparison, students were divided into different score groups. Since, as mentioned in Chapter 1, we adopt the view that students' differences in learning outcomes are related to their different understanding of the subject matter, the differentiation of students into groups was based on their performance in the pre-test rather than on their innate abilities. In each case, students who obtained a score equal to or less than the first quartile in the pre-test was considered to be the "low-score group," whereas those who obtained a score equal to or more than the third quartile in the pre-test were regarded as the "high-score group." Of the high-score group in each study, the performance of the students who had already attained full marks in the pre-test (15–20% of the students in three of the studies and 5% in another five studies) were excluded from the analysis, to avoid the possible ceiling effect on statistical analysis.

A paired *t*-test (one-tailed) at the significance level of 0.05 was also performed in each study, to examine the changes in mean score between the pre-test and the post-test as observed in the high-score group and the low-score group respectively. The null hypothesis used for the whole group in the above comparison was also used for the two score groups, to test for significant improvement in cases when an increase was observed in the mean score in the post-test. However, since the mean score of the high-score group in most studies was already approaching the ceiling and might suffer retrogress, another null hypothesis "the mean score of the high-score group attained in the post-test is equal to or greater than ($\geq$) that in the pre-test" was used for cases in which a decrease was observed in the mean score of the high-score group in the post-test when compared to the pre-test. Thus, if the null hypothesis is rejected, it indicates that the mean score of the high-score group dropped significantly; if it is accepted, it shows that the mean score of the high-score group in the post-test was about the same as or greater than the mean score they obtained in the pre-test.

The results for the two groups are summarized in the following (see also Tables 6.2 and 6.3):

a. In all 27 studies, there was an increase in the mean score of the low-score group in the post-test. These increases were significant on a paired *t*-test (one-tailed) at the significance level of 0.05.

b. In 17 out of the 27 studies, an increase was observed in the mean score of the high-score group in the post-test. The increases in 16 of these studies were significant on a paired *t*-test (one-tailed) at the significance level of 0.05.

c. In 10 out of the 27 studies when a drop was noted in the mean score of the high-score group in the post-test, the drops in five of these studies were not significant on a one-tailed paired *t*-test at the significance level of 0.05.

Table 6.2 A summary of the analysis of the change in mean score of the low-score group in the post-test in each of the 27 Learning Studies carried out during the three academic years

Academic Year	No. of Learning Studies conducted	No. of studies (low-score group)	
		The mean score increased in the post-test	The increase in the mean score in the post-test is significant
2000/01	6	6	6
2001/02	15	15	15
2002/03	6	6	6
Total	27	27	27

(Please refer to Appendix 4 for more detailed information and result of the analysis for each study.)

Table 6.3 A summary of the analysis of the change in mean score of the high-score group in the post-test in each of the 27 Learning Studies carried out during the three academic years

Academic Year	No. of Learning Studies conducted	No. of studies (high-score group)			
		The mean score increased in the post-test	The increase in the mean score is significant	The mean score decreased in the post-test	The decrease in the mean score is NOT significant
2000/01	6	4	4	2	2
2001/02	15	9	8	6	1
2002/03	6	4	4	2	2
Total	27	17	16	10	5

(Please refer to Appendix 4 for more detailed information and result of the analysis for each study.)

Comparisons between the improved scores as measured by the pre-test and post-test across different score groups

It has been shown from the above two types of comparison that, in most of the Learning Studies, significant gain was not only observed at the whole group level but also in both the low-score and high-score groups when their mean scores in the pre-test and post-test were compared. There was also no statistical significant drop in the mean score of the high-score group in many cases when a decrease was observed in the mean score of the high-score group in the post-test when compared to the pre-test. This, however, did not necessarily entail that in most studies the improvement in the mean score of the low-score group was greater than that of the high-score group, or that the difference between the performances of the two groups had been narrowed in the post-test. Therefore, a two-sample t-test (assuming equal variances) at the significance level of 0.05 was further performed on the improved scores (post-test score minus pre-test score) of the low-score group and high-score group of each study. The null hypothesis set for the test was "the improved score obtained by the low-score group is equal to or less than that of the high-score group," and was rejected in 25 out of the 27 studies. This indicated that, in these 25 studies, the improvement made (in actual changed scores) by the low-score group was significantly greater than in the high-score group (see also Table 6.4).

Table 6.4 A summary of the comparison between the improved scores (post-test score minus pre-test score) of the low-score and high-score groups in each of the 27 Learning Studies carried out during the three academic years

Academic year	No. of Learning Studies conducted	No. of studies in which the improved score of the low-score group was significantly greater than that of the high-score group
2000/01	6	5
2001/02	15	14
2002/03	6	6
Total	27	25

(Please refer to Appendix 4 for more detailed information and result of the analysis for each study.)

The above data suggest that, in most of the Learning Studies (24/27), the research lessons did bring a positive effect on the performance of the whole group of students in the area concerned (see Table 6.1). In particular, the low-score group in 25 out of the 27 studies showed significantly better progress than did the high-score group in learning (see Table 6.4). This shows that, in these cases, the two groups were getting closer in acquiring the object of learning. In other words, the difference between the two groups noted in the pre-test was narrowing. Of these 25 studies, 13 appeared not only to

122 *Kwok and Chik*

demonstrate that the difference in the understanding of the subject matter between the low-score and high-score groups was becoming smaller, but also that there was considerable progress made by the whole group as well as the different score groups.

Even so, one may question if the needs of the students in the high-score group were properly addressed in the Learning Studies. It was despite the fact that these students already demonstrated a good mastery of the object of learning in the pre-test, and that in most cases, their performance either increased significantly (16/17) or did not suffer significant decrease (5/10) in the post-test (see Table 6.3). As explained earlier, in catering for individual differences, we believe that students of all abilities should firmly acquire the object of learning that is identified as critical for the students to develop more advanced learning. The research lessons, which focused on specific objects of learning and took the students' ways of seeing particular subject matter as the point of departure, therefore provided a relevance structure or a meaningful context for the students in the high-score group to reinforce and enhance their own understanding of the subject matter. More importantly, these students could clarify the possible misconceptions or recognize the partial or incomplete understanding of the subject matter that they had, which might not have been revealed by the pre-test.

Furthermore, the more able students might have acquired more than the intended object of learning, and what they had actually achieved in the lesson could not be fully reflected in the pre- and post- test comparison but only through in-depth case studies. For example, in a Primary 4 mathematics Learning Study, the students were expected to find the relationship between two distinct yet related concepts of "area" and "perimeter," by means of tabulating different combinations of length and width in calculating the area of a rectangle, given its perimeter, or the perimeter, given its area. Apart from being able to derive the relationship between "area" and "perimeter," some students in the higher ability classes were capable of appreciating the use of systematic tabulation and made unexpected conjectures from their observations. For instance, one of the students in the higher ability class made some interesting discoveries while observing the following table:

Width (cm)	Length (cm)	Perimeter (cm)	Area (cm²)	
1	17	36	17	
2	16	36	32	15
3	15	36	45	13
4	14	36	56	11
5	13	36	65	9
6	12	36	72	7
7	11	36	77	5
8	10	36	80	3
9	9	36	81	1

A. The area increases as the width increases while the length decreases. The more the rectangle is approximately like a square, the larger its area will become.
B. The corresponding length, width, and area are always of the same parity; that is, either they are all even or all odd.
C. A sequence can be obtained by the difference between two consecutive areas (the right-hand column of numbers in the table): 15, 13, 11, 9, 7, 5, 3, 1.

The student further made two interesting conjectures about this sequence:
(a) The first term of the sequence can be obtained by the formula (perimeter ÷ 2) − 3
(b) The number of term in the sequence can be obtained by the formula (perimeter ÷ 4) − 1

There were also some students who noted that the numbers they used for calculation were mostly integers. They wondered what would happen if decimal places were involved and began to grasp the idea of approximation, which was "supposed" to be far too advanced for Primary 4 students. In another Learning Study that focused on developing the students' capability of appreciating and using similes in writing modern Chinese poetry at Primary 6, the teachers noticed that some of the more able students could make use of what they had learnt about simile in reading and writing other genres, in subsequent lessons.

However, caution must be exercised in interpreting the data from the pre- and post-tests. There was no control group to which gain scores could be compared. The idea of having a control group design was rejected fairly early on, based on ethical considerations. It should also be noted that the pre- and post-tests are designed to measure the short-term effect of the research lessons. In the next section, we describe the performance on the Hong Kong Attainment Tests of two groups of students who had attended research lessons in either mathematics or Chinese language throughout the three years of the study, in an attempt to examine the long-term effect of Learning Studies, if any, on student learning, as a form of triangulation.

Triangulation with the Hong Kong Attainment Tests

In this section, we discuss the analysis of the Hong Kong Attainment Tests (HKAT) as a source of triangulation. The HKAT are administered by the Hong Kong government to all students in Hong Kong at the end of each school year, in the subjects of Chinese language, English language, and mathematics. The tests are designed to assist schools in diagnosing students' progress in learning and in monitoring the standards of the three subjects across years within each level. The test papers are revised every year. To facilitate schools' diagnoses, the government uses sample data from the HKAT to compile norm tables which provide the whole range of students' raw scores, standardized scores, and their relative standings in the distribution annually. For valid comparison of students' performance in different tests, the standardized scores are transformed from the raw scores on a common scale with reference to the performance of other students of the same level in the whole territory, and are expressed with a mean equivalent to 100. In other words, students scoring above 100 in the standardized score are above the average standard. Students scoring below 100 are below the average standard.

The analysis of the HKAT reported in the following sections was thus based on the standardized scores the same group of students attained in the respective subject (Chinese language/mathematics) that their school (School 1/2) specialized in when conducting Learning Studies. The data were collected for the academic years 1999/2000 (Primary 3), 2000/01 (Primary 4), 2001/02 (Primary 5) and 2002/03 (Primary 6), and the standardized scores in 1999/2000 were used as a baseline when no intervention (Learning Study) took place.

The Hong Kong Attainment Tests in Chinese language

School 1 specialized in conducting Learning Studies in Chinese language during the three years of implementation (2000–03). However, the data of two out of five classes collected from the school in electronic copy were found to be erroneous: the input of the raw scores for the two classes in 1999/2000 was the same as it was in 2000/01. Unfortunately, the school had to report the loss of the data of these two classes. Also, according to the school, the data submitted to the external evaluation team of the study were limited to two of the other three classes, whereas those to the government were only a random sample of the students. As no full set of reliable data was ascertainable for the two classes, they were excluded from the analysis. In one of the three classes that was included in the analysis, there was a change of teachers in each year of the study, i.e., the class was taught by three teachers over the three-year period of the study.

Comparison was made between the mean scores of two groups of students (the whole group of students at the year level, and the low-achieving group of students who obtained a standardized score of less than 80 in 1999/2000). These were also compared with the means of the norm (100). The purpose of comparing the mean scores of each year with the norm data was to trace the change in students' attainment. In order to examine whether the variation in attainment had narrowed or widened, the standard deviations of the two groups in each year of study were also compared. The results are summarized as follows:

- The pattern of change in average standardized score for the whole group and the low-achieving group in School 1 was similar: an increase was observed for each group in each year when compared with the baseline data for each group (1999/2000). In addition, their mean scores were approaching or performing slightly better than the mean of the norm (see Figure 6.1). A paired *t*-test (one-tailed) was also employed to test for level of significance of the changes in the average standardized scores of both groups in School 1 in each of the years 2000/01, 2001/02, 2002/03 as compared to the baseline data. The increases in the first two years for the two groups were found to be significant, and the p value was smaller than 0.05.

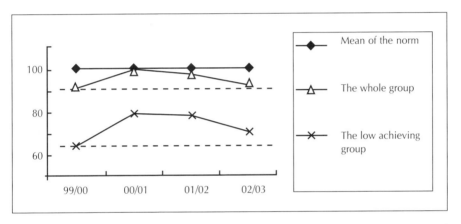

Figure 6.1 The pattern of change in average standardized score for the whole group and the low-achieving group in School 1 (HKAT — Chinese language)

The pattern of change in standard deviation, however, differed between the whole group and the low-achieving groups in School 1 (see Figure 6.2). The variation in standardized score among the whole group became narrower after the three years of study, whereas that among the low-achieving group widened, meaning that some students in the low-achieving group had actually improved considerably. For example, of the 11 out of 17 students who scored less than 80 in the standardized score in 1999/2000, the gain in standardized scores varied from 5 to 25.73 in 02/03.

The analysis was also triangulated with the number of Learning Studies on Chinese language carried out in School 1 as well as the foci of the studies. Table 6.5 summarizes the information.

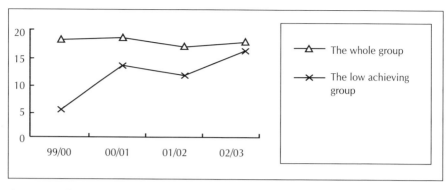

Figure 6.2 The pattern of change in standard deviation for the whole group and the low-achieving group in School 1 (HKAT — Chinese language)

Table 6.5 Summary of the number of Learning Studies and their foci in each year of the study and the corresponding average standardized score attained by three out of five classes of students in School 1 in HKAT (Chinese language)

Academic Year (year of study)	Focus of Learning Study (number of studies carried out)	HKAT — Chinese Language (Standardized Score)	
		Whole group (n=71)	
		Average	Change from baseline data
1999/2000 (baseline)	—	91.17	—
2000/01 (year 1)	Text comprehension (2: one in each term)	100.28	+9.11 *
	Writing: Modern Poetry (1: in 2nd term)		
2001/02 (year 2)	Text comprehension (1: in 1st term)	97.72	+6.55 *
	Writing: Simile (1: 2nd term)		
2002/03 (year 3)	Writing: Simile in modern poetry (1: 2nd term)	92.50	+1.33 *
		Group of students with standardized scores less than 80 in 99/00 (n=17)	
1999/2000 (baseline)	—	64.55	—
2000/01 (year 1)	Text comprehension (2: one in each term)	79.13	+14.58 *
	Writing: Modern Poetry (1: in 2nd term)		
2001/02 (year 2)	Text comprehension (1: in 1st term)	78.31	+13.76 *
	Writing: Simile (1: 2nd term)		
2002/03 (year 3)	Writing: Simile in modern poetry (1: 2nd term)	70.52	+5.97 *

* The increases noted in this year of study, when compared with the baseline, were significant on a one-tailed *t*-test at the significance level of 0.05.

From Table 6.5, we see that the change in the average standardized scores for both groups in School 1 seems to be associated with the foci and the number of Learning Studies conducted:

1. Relatively higher average standardized scores were observed in the years 2000/01 and 2001/02, when there were two Learning Studies and one Learning Study respectively focusing on text comprehension.
2. The biggest gain in average standardized score was observed in the year 2000/01, when the largest number of Learning Studies was carried out.
3. Comparatively higher average standardized scores were attained in the years when more Learning Studies were spaced out throughout the academic year.
4. The gains in the average scores, compared to the baseline scores, of the group of low-achieving students were higher than the gains in the average scores of the whole group throughout the three years of the study.

One possible explanation for the observation in the first point here might have to do with the nature of the test items of the HKAT in Chinese language. The test measures students' attainment in four main areas, namely, reading, writing, speaking, and listening. The texts used in the reading tests were of a similar style to the texts chosen for the Learning Studies. However, the writing tests required students to write on a certain topic in particular genres (e.g., letter writing and narration). The effect of the studies that focused on writing modern poetry and the use of a particular rhetoric — simile — therefore could not be reflected in the HKAT.

The observations made in the second and third points might reflect the effect of the research lessons.

In the fourth point, the fact that the low-achieving group gained more in standardized score on average than did the whole group from 1999/2000 to 2002/03 also seems to suggest a greater effect of the study in helping this group of students to learn more effectively.

As aforementioned, there was a change of teachers in one of the three classes. This might actually have affected the students' learning both generally and specifically in the research lessons. We noticed that the loss of the teacher (a very good teacher who made valuable and significant input to the Learning Study group) after the first year of the project affected the group dynamic. This in turn affected the quality of the subsequent Learning Studies. We suspect that the learning of the other two classes, in which there was no change in teacher, would also be affected indirectly. Therefore, in order to examine the teacher effect on student learning, comparison was made between the patterns of change in mean standardized score of the class (Class A) in which there were changes in teachers and that of the two classes (Classes B and C) that had no change in teacher throughout the three years of implementation. A one-tailed paired *t*-test at the significance level of 0.05 was also performed on the changes in mean standardized score between the baseline and each academic year, and between academic years. The analysis was done only at the whole group level since students in the low-achieving group were in Class B or Class C. The results are summarized as follows (see also Figures 6.3 and 6.4):

- In Class A, in which there were changes in teachers in the first two years of study, after the surge in mean standardized score from 1999/2000 to 2000/01, a decrease was observed from 2000/01 to 2001/02 as well as from 2001/02 to 2002/03. Whereas the increases in 2000/01 and 2001/02 as compared with the baseline in 1999/2000 were significant on a one-tailed paired *t*-test at the significance level of 0.05, the mean standardized score in the last year of study actually dropped below the baseline, and the drop was significant. The decreases observed from 2000/01 to 2001/02 and from 2001/02 to 2002/03 were also significant.
- In Classes B and C, in which there was NO change in teacher throughout the study, a similar pattern was observed: there was a large increase from 1999/2000 to 2000/01, and decreases were noted between 2000/01 and 2001/02, and between 2001/02 and 2002/03. Whereas the increases in each year as compared with the baseline in 1999/2000 were significant on a one-tailed paired *t*-test at the significance level of 0.05, the drops from 2000/01 to 2001/02 and from 2001/02 to 02/03 were not significant.

The result thus seems to confirm our suspicion about a possible "teacher effect."

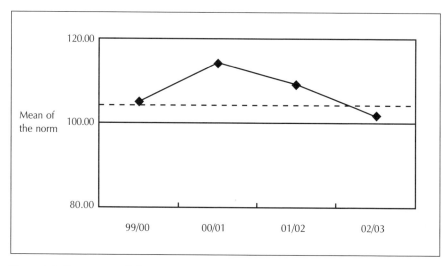

Figure 6.3 The pattern of change in mean standardized score of Class A in which there was a change in teacher in the first two years of study

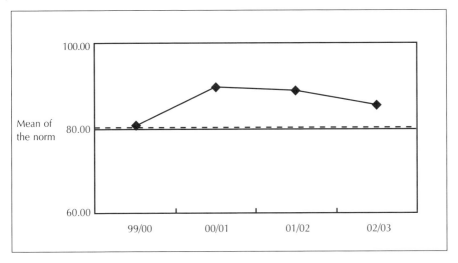

Figure 6.4 The pattern of change in mean standardized score of Classes B and C in which there was NO change in teacher in the first two years of study

The Hong Kong Attainment Tests in mathematics

The same analysis was performed on the data collected on the HKAT in mathematics attained by two groups of students (the whole group and the low-achieving group) in School 2, which specialized in doing Learning Studies in mathematics during the three years of implementation (2000–03). The findings are summarized as follows:

- As shown in Figure 6.5, for the whole group of students, the average standardized scores showed little significant change for the years 2000/01 and 2001/02, but a more marked increase was observed in the third year of study approaching the norm (the p value being smaller than 0.05 calculated using a one-tailed paired t-test). Also, there was a statistically significant increase in the average standardized scores of the low-achieving group throughout the three years when compared with the baseline data (the p values being smaller than 0.05 calculated using a one-tailed paired t-test), and the scores gradually moved towards the norm.
- The significant increase in the standard deviation of the low-achieving group from 1999/2000 to 2002/03 means that the difference in achievement in the group widened, i.e., some students in the group had actually improved considerably after the three years of study. Twenty-six out of 39 students who scored less than 80 in the standardized score in 1999/2000 showed gains in scores from 1.18 to 38.69 in 2002/03.

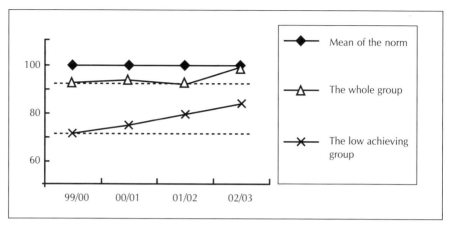

Figure 6.5 The pattern of change in average standardized score for the whole group and the low-achieving group in School 2 (HKAT — mathematics)

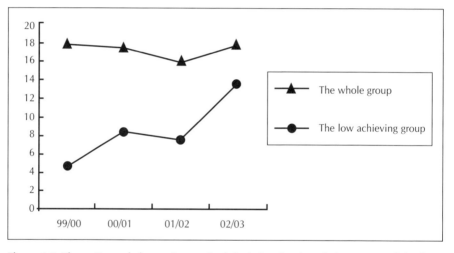

Figure 6.6 The pattern of change in standard deviation for the whole group and the low-achieving group in School 2 (HKAT in mathematics)

The analysis was also triangulated with the number of Learning Studies on mathematics conducted in the school and the foci of each Learning Study. Table 6.6 summarizes this information.

Unlike in Chinese language, we do not expect that the effect of the Learning Studies in mathematics can be reflected in the HKAT in such a short time. In the HKAT, students are tested on particular mathematical concepts and related operational skills in the five domains: number, shape and space, measurement, data handling, and algebra. The Learning Studies that were carried out covered only a very small area in some of these domains.

Table 6.6 Summary of the foci and number of Learning Studies carried out in each year of study and the corresponding average standardized score attained by all five classes of students in School 2 in HKAT (mathematics)

Academic Year (year of study)	Focus of Learning Study (number of studies carried out)	HKAT — Mathematics (Standardized Score)	
		Whole group (n=136)	
		Average	Change from baseline data
1999/2000 (baseline)	—	93.63	—
2000/01 (year 1)	Number: Unit and Unitising of fractions (1: 1st term)	93.94	+0.31
	Shape and Space: Area and Perimeter (1: in 2nd term)		
2001/02 (year 2)	Shape and Space: Area of parallelograms (1: in 1st term)	92.79	-0.84
	Shape and Space: Volume of cube and cuboid (1: 2nd term)		
2002/03 (year 3)	Measures: Speed (1: 2nd term)	99.01	+5.38 *
		Scored less than 80 in standardized score in 99/00 (n=39)	
1999/2000 (baseline)	—	71.63	—
2000/01 (year 1)	Number: Unit and Unitising of fractions (1: 1st term)	74.00	+2.37*
	Shape and Space: Area and Perimeter (1: in 2nd term)		
2001/02 (year 2)	Shape and Space: Area of parallelograms (1: in 1st term)	77.43	+5.80*
	Shape and Space: Volume of cube and cuboid (1: 2nd term)		
2002/03 (year 3)	Measures: Speed (1: 2nd term)	80.21	+8.58*

* The increases noted in this year of study, when compared with the baseline, were significant on a one-tailed t-test at the significance level of 0.05.

Also, some of the concepts and the related operational skills involved in certain domains are closely related to those of other domains. For example, the concepts of area, perimeter, and volume and the related operational skills (shape and space) that we dealt with in three Learning Studies in the first two years are interrelated, and to a certain extent also related to the proportional thinking (number) developed in the first study carried out in the year 2000/01. The study in the last year was also about proportion in the context of measuring speed (measures). It would therefore take time for the various critical aspects to be better developed and for a wider coverage of specific concepts in various domains to be achieved before the effect of the Learning Studies can be reflected in the attainment tests.

Seen from this light, the relatively larger increases observed in average standardized score for both groups in School 2 between 1999/2000 and 2002/03 could be attributed to the fact that there was a wider coverage of concepts in various domains by 2002/03 than in the beginning years.

The low-achieving students in School 2 also showed a larger gain than the whole group in the attainment tests in mathematics throughout the three years of study (see Table 6.6).

However, the use of the HKAT as a sole measure of the effect of the study's approach on student learning has to be taken with caution. Since each Learning Study focused only on a particular object of learning, and students were only taught one or two research lessons in a year, it is not realistic to expect that these research lessons would have a great effect on the result of the HKAT, which is not designed to measure the students' learning of what the research lessons focused on. However, when this is considered together with the findings using the gain in post-test compared with the pre-test in the Learning Studies, as described in the previous sections, the result takes on significance.

Conclusion

In this chapter, we presented the comprehensive results of the pre- and post-test data of the 27 Learning Studies conducted within the research project. The result seems to support our discussions in earlier chapters that Learning Study, which is premised on three types of variation focusing on specific objects of learning (see Chapter 3, pp. 29–32), is a useful tool for teachers in helping students of different abilities to learn the specific area covered in mainstream schools. The findings of the analysis triangulating the number and foci of the Learning Studies with the HKAT data across the three years of study also suggest a positive relationship between conducting Learning Studies and students' achievement in the long run. This means that, the more Learning Studies that can address the critical aspects of the measurement areas in the attainment tests, the better the students can achieve in those tests. In both analyses, we found that the gain in scores of the lower score group is higher than in the higher score group or the whole group over the three years of study. These results, when triangulated, enable us to be optimistic that we have found a way to cater for individual differences.

7

Drawing Insights from the "Catering for Individual Differences: Building on Variation" Project

LO Mun Ling

Introduction

Have we been successful at developing a strategy to cater for individual differences? We believe that we have succeeded in pointing out a direction, even if we have not had sufficient success in solving the problem once and for all. Our work over the three years of the project confirms that critical differences exist between different students' ways of seeing most of the things that they are expected to learn about in school. Above all, there are critical differences between the students' intuitive understanding and the understanding that is embodied in the notations and concepts of schools, which have caused many students to fail in school. If we are serious about catering for individual differences, and really determined to enable each student to learn, then we must identify and address these differences. In the previous chapters, we showed how we tried to accomplish this. However, it is not an easy task; neither is there an instant solution. We need to work on the curriculum, pedagogy, assessment, and teacher empowerment simultaneously. Learning Study, which is based on the conceptual framework of variation, has proved to be a powerful tool. Below we discuss the effect of our study.

Advancing the professional knowledge base of teaching

Improving the curriculum

In Hong Kong, the majority of primary school teachers are non-graduates who obtained their certificate in education through sub-degree programmes. The length of such programmes does not allow them to develop a substantive knowledge base of their teaching subjects and a sound knowledge of the curriculum. In many schools, teachers also have to teach subjects that they are not trained in. Thus, these teachers tend to be reliant on textbooks.

Unfortunately, we often find a lack of coherence or internal logic in the sequencing of some of the topics in textbooks. For example, in the learning of fractions, the concepts of units and unitizing are very important. Yet these are inadequately dealt with in most textbooks. In the Learning Study on water, students were confused by the use of the same term "水蒸氣" (water vapour) for steam (issuing from boiling water), water vapour (issuing from hot water) that is visible, and water in the gaseous state that is not visible. In the Learning Study on the colour of light, both teachers and students were misled by the reference to the "seven" colours of the rainbow, as a rainbow shows a spectrum of colours and not only seven of them. Our Learning Studies throw light on how student difficulties in learning these concepts can be identified and dealt with in each teaching unit, and how the curriculum can be better organized, structured, and modified to help students learn more deeply and effectively. Also, the limited resource provided by a textbook is not adequate for achieving certain chosen objects of learning. For example, in the Learning Study in Primary 4 Chinese language, which was about modern poetry (in the year 2000/01), many additional modern poems written by Chinese children were used as supplementary material. These poems were chosen to create the variation necessary for students to discern the common critical aspects of modern poetry.

Teachers in the Learning Study groups developed more confidence in deviating from their textbooks. The object of learning in each Learning Study was very carefully chosen. These objects of learning were chosen because they were worthwhile capabilities to be developed; for example, the capability to understand certain concepts that were so difficult that they often presented themselves as obstacles to further learning for many students. The teachers were not satisfied with simply teaching facts or superficial understanding. They ventured into the arena of higher order thinking skills and deeper appreciation of the disciplines.

Many students get by in school and may even obtain a university degree without really understanding what they are supposed to learn. Does it matter? Initially, we pointed out that we believe that one of the most important forms of learning is learning that affects our way of seeing, and that one of the most important purposes of schooling is to help children see the world in more powerful ways. Gardner (1991) says it very well: "The understandings of the disciplines represent the most important cognitive achievements of human beings. It is necessary to come to know these understandings if we are to be fully human, to live in our time, to be able to understand it to the best of our abilities, and to build upon it" (p. 11). That is how civilization spreads and advances. Also, learning how to think requires common sense to be challenged. Understanding a discipline is a stepping-stone to developing that discipline and challenging orthodoxy.

Our recommendations:

- Schools are increasingly vested with the responsibility to develop their own school-based curriculum to cater for their own students' needs. We believe that any curriculum materials used and the way the curriculum is structured should be based on research that takes into consideration how students learn. Learning Studies will contribute to school-based curriculum development by informing what the worthwhile objects of learning are, what the critical aspects of these objects of learning are, which of these are pre-requisite knowledge, and how the different objects of learning should be structured. Textbooks should be regarded as only one resource among many.

- We believe that it is more likely for schools to succeed if they take an evolutionary approach to curriculum design. This can be done by setting up Learning Study teams within the school. Initially, teachers can start with one lesson in their textbook. When teachers are capable of teaching one lesson which embodies the worthwhile goals of education, the essence of the discipline or subject, good elements of teaching and learning, effective assessment as feedback to teaching and learning, then they are ready to proceed to work on a curriculum unit, followed by the curriculum for a whole year level, and later, the curriculum for the whole primary school level. This approach is even more important in developing cross-curricular themes or new curricula in the Key Learning Areas or integrated subjects, to avoid loss of the essence of the discipline and subject depth.

- To hasten the process, the Learning Study team in each school, while continuing to work on further cycles of their research lessons year after year and to become an expert team in this aspect, can share with other Learning Study teams in other schools, thus contributing to the development of a learning community.

Advancing knowledge on how to use variation as a guiding principle of pedagogical design

Intuitive ideas are difficult to alter. As we demonstrated in the case of water (Chapter 2, pp. 13–4), Student A could easily repeat what Ms W told her without making any mistakes, and she would easily pass in an examination. However, her intuitive understanding persisted when she had to explain her everyday experience, e.g., why there is water on her plastic bottle. This makes a strong case that teaching by simply telling may not result in learning, especially when it involves the understanding of a concept. We cannot make students understand a concept. We can only make it possible for them to focus on all the critical aspects simultaneously, hoping that they can discern for themselves and arrive at a new way of seeing. But, if the necessary conditions for discernment are absent, it is impossible for students to learn. Through the Learning Studies, we have developed and enhanced our knowledge of using variation as a guiding principle of pedagogical design to cater for students' differences. By carefully analysing each research lesson to compare the teaching acts and student learning outcomes, we discovered how different patterns of variation make different kinds of learning possible. We have now come to a better understanding of how to bring about certain kinds of learning. However, more work needs to be done in the analysis of data to develop a deeper understanding about the nature of such learning.

Our recommendations:

• More Learning Studies should be conducted to discover necessary patterns of variation to help students learn more effectively and reach their potential, and how these patterns can be applied in different subject areas.

Advancing understanding of assessment for learning

The curriculum reform encourages the use of diagnostic assessment and assessment for learning. In our Learning Studies, the assessment items that teachers developed for the pre- and post-tests demonstrated clearly how teachers have advanced in their understanding of diagnostic assessment and assessment for learning. When teachers developed a clear understanding of the purpose of assessment and what they were in fact assessing, they also developed a clearer understanding of what they were intending to teach for the benefit of students.

Assessment for learning featured very strongly in Learning Studies. Through careful analysis of lessons, by observation or using video recordings, teachers were sensitized to their students' different ways of understanding and the difficulties they experienced during the lesson. This information was then fed into the next cycle of research lessons. Such a procedure provides an additional means of using assessment to improve teaching and learning; it also demonstrates how peer observation can be fully made use of for improving both teaching and student learning.

The results of the post-tests were very carefully analysed and related to the teaching act. In this way, teachers were able to obtain feedback on the effect of their teaching on student learning.

Our recommendations:

• The conceptual framework based on variation provides a powerful tool for setting assessment items. Exercises and tests should be reconceptualized as diagnostic tools to help teachers to identify their students' difficulties, help them in planning more effective teaching, and to give feedback to students about their learning, as well as informing the teachers' own teaching.

- The Learning Study model can be adopted in schools that wish to use peer observation for staff development purposes. This model highlights the importance of learning from students and from other teachers before, during, and after the observed lesson.

Providing an alternative perspective on student learning and catering for individual differences

In Chapter 6, we showed that Learning Study has a positive effect on students' learning outcomes. If the project is able to cater for individual differences, then we should expect all students would be able to achieve the object of learning. We were excited to find that, in all Learning Studies, the lower academic achieving group showed significantly greater improvement in actual gain scores than did the higher academic achieving group in 25 out of 27 cases. This finding was more significant when triangulated with the Hong Kong Attainment Tests. We found that the standardized scores of the lower achieving group increased continuously throughout the three years of study in both schools, and the data of the standard deviation of the two groups showed that the difference between the two groups became narrower.

Some people may wonder how such an effect on the students could be possible, given that they experienced only one or two research lessons per year. We believe that the result supports our belief that the research lessons helped to remove obstacles to learning and developed in students more powerful ways of seeing, so that they were able to continue to learn. Another reason may be that teachers are empowered, so that they can, in their everyday teaching, make use of what they have learnt in Learning Study, to identify worthwhile objects of learning and their related critical aspects, and are able to make use of variation as a guiding principle of pedagogical design to help their students focus on these critical aspects. This view is supported by the data from teacher interviews.

Our recommendations:

There is no quick-fix solution or foolproof curriculum. The only way to catering for individual differences is to recognize that teaching is a professional activity. One possible solution is to facilitate Learning Studies and to share the results among teachers.

Empowerment of teachers

We have shown that Learning Study has proven to be a powerful tool for teachers' professional development. When the teachers were supported in a learning community, as in the Learning Study team, they made great advances in their knowledge of the subject as well as in their understanding of students and teaching skills, through engaging in action research cycles and peer observations.

In the past, the weak subject knowledge displayed by many teachers was attributed to their low qualifications. It was believed that requiring all teachers to be degree holders of relevant subjects would solve the problem. There is plenty of evidence in the literature telling us that this is not enough. For one thing, we have many studies showing us that even university students do not really "understand" the subjects that they have learnt. Also, we have Ma's (1999) study showing us that the sample of US mathematics teachers in the study, who were university graduates, had very little understanding of the fundamental mathematics they taught at primary schools. In China, the sample of teachers in Ma's study, who had received only twelve years of schooling, about six years less than their counterparts in the US, showed profound understanding of fundamental mathematics, and taught in ways that encouraged deep conceptual understanding rather than simply transmitting procedural knowledge. Our own study also shows that, even teachers who did not have a science background, after the Learning Study, gained enough conceptual understanding of the science in the topic they were teaching that they taught just as well as the other teachers who did have such a background (see Chapter 4).

Before we can recruit teachers who are really masters of their own subjects, Learning Study is a powerful way to help teachers to be competent in what they teach. We cannot turn a teacher into an expert in a subject within a short time, but we can help the teacher to become competent to teach a particular object of learning in class, through a Learning Study. Some people may query the cost-effectiveness of Learning Study. However, as has been demonstrated in our study, the effect on the teachers was profound, and what they learnt from the Learning Study was transferred to their everyday teaching.

Our recommendations:

- We recommend that every teacher in Hong Kong should have the opportunity to engage in a Learning Study at least once every three years as a core component of continuing professional development programmes, and to share the experience with other teachers. Teachers should also be able to attend sharing seminars of other Learning Study teams, which may focus on different objects of learning. As there are hundreds of schools in Hong Kong, very soon, we would have adequate cover for every topic in the curriculum that presents difficulties for students to learn. Teaching will then become a much more professional activity.

- We believe that it would be useful for student teachers to be inducted into Learning Study during the initial teacher education programmes, thus equipping them with a tool for continuing professional development throughout their career.

The way forward

Learning Study is a very labour-intensive and expensive activity. It involves teachers working together as partners with academics/researchers over a long period, gathering data about their students and their own teaching, studying and analysing the topic very carefully, planning and evaluating. However, compared to the large amount of resources that have been poured into curriculum reforms, and the minimal effects such reforms have in affecting student learning outcomes and teaching practice (Hattie, 1999; Wang, Walberg and Haertel, 1993; Sipe and Curletter, 1997; Cuban, 1990; Tyack and Cuban, 1995; Morris, 2000; Pong and Morris, 2002), Learning Study is in fact very cost-effective.

Is it possible to involve more schools in participating in high-quality Learning Studies? Our experience tells us that it is. With the knowledge gained through working with the two project schools, we have used examples from the Learning Studies to run workshops, seminars, and training courses for teachers. Through a government-funded Progressive and Innovative Primary Schools Project, we have supported Learning Studies in over forty primary schools. These second-generation Learning Studies, which are supported by academics we have influenced and teacher development consultants whom we have trained, are of high quality. Equally encouraging is the fact that all participating teachers invariably demonstrated considerable professional growth after going through the process.

Through the project, we have gained much knowledge about the implementation of Learning Studies in schools. Below, we suggest conditions that would favour its implementation.

Recommendations for adapting the strategy in schools:

Conditions for initiation
- Before initiating Learning Study in schools, teachers should be well prepared by first attending some courses on Learning Study or some Learning Study seminars, to become familiar with the idea and concepts,

and fully understand the implications for their workload and their own involvement, before committing themselves.

- A group of teachers who show the greatest enthusiasm should be supported to participate in the Learning Study first. The subject or level is not an important factor. It is important to avoid involving teachers who are unwilling, and not to try starting too many Learning Studies at once as a trial.

Creation of a supportive environment in the school

- Schools should create the infrastructure to facilitate teachers engaging in Learning Studies. This may involve rearranging timetables to enable teachers of the same subjects to have free periods together so that they can have a convenient meeting time. Heads can make use of the government's Capacity Enhancement Grant or other available resources (e.g., QEF) to employ extra teachers to relieve the workload of those teachers engaged in Learning Studies. Each Learning Study takes an average of three months to complete. The extra human resources may be shared by various subject groups over the year.
- When the Learning Study is successful, the experience can be shared with the whole school. Teachers who emerge as leaders can then lead other Learning Study groups.
- The criteria for success should not be based only on students' learning outcomes. Other indicators like the quality of the resulting curriculum, effect on teachers' development, and insights drawn should be considered.
- The success of the Learning Study should be regarded as the effort of the whole team. Associating it with appraisal of individual teachers' performance should be avoided.

Connecting to a professional network

- Heads should set up an intra-school infrastructure for sharing and scrutinizing research lessons, so that teachers from various Learning Study teams can learn from each other and improve.
- It is equally important that teachers should participate in inter-school networks through participating/presenting their work in public Learning Study seminars.

Partnership with higher education institutes as a resource in time and expertise

- The support of academics from a higher education institute is desirable, especially during the initial stages of implementation of Learning Study. The expertise from each party is essential to the success of the research lesson. Academics are close to the research literature and are experts in the pedagogical content knowledge of their own subjects. Thus they can help teachers save considerable time by avoiding reinventing the wheel.
- Schools should take seriously their partnership with teacher education

providers, so that both can benefit from the partnership. By taking in large numbers of student teachers of the same subject for block practicum, schools can release a large number of teachers of the same subject to do Learning Studies over the practicum period, which usually lasts for about six to eight weeks. While the student teachers are in the schools, schools can negotiate the involvement of their subject supervisors in the Learning Studies. Such resources in time and expertise are free.

Recommendations for strategies of dissemination and teacher professional development:

- Teachers should be encouraged to engage in Learning Studies as an integral part of their own professional development. In future, when there is a policy requiring teachers to undertake continuing professional development work, the time they engage in Learning Study should be counted towards the required number of hours.
- There should be venues for inter-school sharing, so that the quality of research lessons can be publicly scrutinized and shared, thus encouraging excellence in practice. This can easily be done by linking up with higher education institutes or regional education offices that are interested in running dissemination seminars to promote good practices. Resource schools, where the practice of doing Learning Studies has been well established, can also be set up to act as bases for the promotion and dissemination of good practices in carrying out Learning Studies. An award for high-quality Learning Studies may also be established.
- As Learning Study helps to sensitize teachers to all aspects of teaching and learning and to what a good lesson means, and can help teachers to develop a research stance to teaching so that they can continue to learn and improve, we believe that it would be a good idea to make Learning Study a core element of pre-service, in-service, and continuous professional development programmes for teachers. It would also be beneficial for providers of mentoring courses to make Learning Study an integral part, as it helps to develop some of the essential skills, e.g., conferencing skills, ability to observe and analyse lessons, and the capability to assess how the teaching enactment affects students' learning outcomes.
- Reforms that take a revolutionary approach often fail because they blame teachers and past systems for the failure of schooling and ask teachers to throw away what they already know and can do well in order to try some other innovative strategies. Learning study provides an alternative: an evolutionary approach to curriculum reform. In Learning Study, we value teachers' experience and contributions. They work in a supportive

learning community that values each other's expertise and experience, where the focus is on the object of learning and not on the failures of individuals. Teamwork is valued. The success of any Learning Study is attributed to the success of the whole team, and every member shares the glory and joy equally. Thus it encourages collaboration and team spirit, and nurtures the learning community in schools instead of celebrating the success of individual teachers.

- This project is one example of how close partnership among the Curriculum Development Institute, higher education institutes, and schools can work very well. Such a model of collaboration should be encouraged in future.

Conclusion

In Chapter 3, we stated our main research question as follows:

Is it feasible to use Learning Study, which is premised on the three types of variation, to help to cater for individual differences in mainstream schools?

In particular, we seek to answer the following more specific questions:
1. Can worthwhile objects of learning that are fundamental to students' learning be identified?
2. Can critical aspects of these intended objects of learning be found?
3. Can teachers make use of different patterns of variation to help students of different abilities grasp the critical aspect(s) identified for their learning of a particular object of learning?
4. Are the participating teachers empowered to cater for individual differences using the three types of variation through engaging in Learning Studies?
5. What are the contributing and hindering factors to the project's implementation?

The answer to the first four questions is obviously "yes." We have also made recommendations on how Learning Study can be successfully implemented in schools.

In our project, we have tried to find ways to cater for individual differences in the form of differences in students' learning outcomes. We have pointed the way to how it is possible to do this by making use of Learning Study as a tool. In the previous sections, we have demonstrated how critical differences in students' understanding of specific subject matter can be identified and dealt with. However, we must caution that the search for such differences is just the beginning and not the end at the completion of a Learning Study.

For any chosen object of learning, the search for students' different ways of understanding which may cause difficulties in learning can only stop when we have exhausted all variations in children's understanding that present themselves as obstacles to acquiring particular object of learning. In each cycle of research lesson on a particular object of learning, we will discover some aspects that are critical, and we can improve the learning of a number of students. Even when we are able to raise the percentage of students who can demonstrate good grasp of the object of learning up to 95%, we should still not be satisfied. We should continue to ask: What about the five percent that are still unable to learn? What critical aspects have we missed? The ultimate target is to enable *each and every one* to be able to grasp the concepts, if they are important concepts or capabilities for further studies in the curriculum.

As our project embraces a qualitative approach, and the main data sets are case studies, we aim at giving descriptive accounts and interpretation of cases, which allow teachers to draw useful insights that can be applied to their own classroom situations. We must caution against judging the success or failure of Learning Study by solely comparing students' pre and post-test results. Such data are mainly for diagnostic and triangulation purposes. They are also intended for use by teachers to make the connection between their teaching act and student learning outcomes. The major contribution of our project is in the insights that can be drawn on all aspects of education: curriculum making, pedagogy, assessment, changing school culture, and teachers' professional development. Only when we have made significant improvements in the above can we make similar improvements in student learning. The project has also contributed greatly to the development of the Theory of Variation, in particular, informing about the functions of different patterns of variation, and field-testing its use in different subjects.

We strongly believe that when the significant contribution of Learning Study is recognized and becomes an integral part of teacher education programmes, mentoring training courses, teachers' continuing professional development programmes, and reform effort, then we would be able to make significant progress in dealing with the variations in student learning outcomes.

8

Conclusion: For Each and Everyone

LO Mun Ling and Ference MARTON

In this book, we wanted to share the ideas underlying an attempt to cater for individual differences and ideas about the ways in which this attempt was realized.

The phrase "catering for individual differences" refers to the observation that, when all students are taught in the same way, they learn different things and they master to different extents that which they are expected to learn. When they have to deal with the next aspect/area, they must rely on what they have learnt previously. So, the likelihood of ending up with differences between the students becomes increasingly large for each new topic. This is one of the mechanisms through which some students become "good students" and other students become "weak students."

From the teacher's point of view the situation looks like this: "I am facing a class of students in which the prerequisites for learning vary considerably. And I can teach only one way at a time. But if I teach in one way, different students will learn differently, some will succeed and some will fail. If some fail, I fail." A research project called "Catering for Individual Differences" should have something to offer to this teacher. In fact, the following is what we have to offer.

Learning is always the learning of *something*. When you are good at learning, you are good at learning *something*. You are good at learning how to express yourself when writing in Chinese or speaking English, how to make sense of fluctuations in the price of goods, how to compute the area of a piece of land, to understand why your car is using more fuel when you drive faster, and why the spaceship is not using any fuel at all on its way to Venus after it has left the gravitational field of the Earth, etc. The learning of any specific capability (knowledge or skill) is highly affected by the specific way in which that particular capability is taught.

So, learning in school is very much the learning of all the specific things that are taught there. Being good at learning is being good at learning all those specific things, and being good at teaching is being good at teaching all those specific things. Accordingly, if you want to improve your teaching, you have to pay attention to every specific thing that you teach. You have to find out what difficulties the students may have with each particular item that you teach and find a way by which it can be taught in a powerful way.

But if this is the case, why is it that teachers are very rarely talked about by how they teach particular topics? Teachers are talked about almost without exception in general terms such as "good," "nice," "funny," "strict," "tough," "weak," etc., i.e., in the terms in which we talk about people in general. As Lortie (1975) points out, in the industrialized world, basically everyone has been in the physical proximity of different teachers, teaching different things, for ten to twelve years. So why is it that their particular ways of teaching specific things is hardly ever noticed, and even less talked about?

The reason is, we believe, that there are very few people who have seen two or more teachers teach the same thing. And, according to the very theory made use of in the studies described in this book, in order to notice differences in teaching something, that something must remain invariant while the ways of teaching it varies.

The Learning Study is an arrangement for doing this. Some of the characteristic features of the Learning Study are as follows.

- Teachers focus on the object of learning;
- learn from learners in trying to find out the nature of their potential difficulties with the object of learning in question;
- work with other teachers and learn from them;
- try to find ways in which they can contribute to creating the necessary conditions for the expected learning to occur, by drawing on a relevant theory of learning;
- find out the outcome of the attempt and thereby receive feedback, i.e., information about the effects of their acts.

This approach takes learning (and not teaching) as its point of departure, it gives space to the learners for making choices, making judgements, and making use of their own ideas. At the same time, it does not hand over all the responsibility to the students. The teacher must ascertain that the necessary conditions for the learners' discernment of critical aspects/features are constituted in the classroom, mainly thanks to what he or she does in teaching.

Judging from what was said above in this book, participation in Learning Studies was found to be an excellent form of in-service training, according to the teachers themselves. But did the students gain from their teachers' professional development? Table 6.5 on p. 126 and Table 6.6 on p. 131 demonstrate remarkable improvement in the HKAT scores in Chinese language and mathematics classes participating in the study. As the students' participation was restricted to one or a few lessons per term, it does not seem very likely that the improvement was directly related to what they learnt during those lessons. As pointed out on p. 127, it seems much more likely that the improvement in student learning was due to the indirect effect of the teachers' participation in the study. In doing Learning Study, the teachers seemed to have changed their way of approaching the lessons subsequently and thus brought about a general improvement in the achievement of their students. In fact, we also have substantial data on the direct effects of students' participation in the studies, on their learning outcomes. Positive differences between post-test and pre-test indicate that students have learnt what they were expected to learn to an observable extent. And this we found to be the case, basically every time. However, as there were no non-participating classes to compare with, we cannot claim that students participating in Learning Studies learnt more about the object of learning than students who were taught the same object of learning, but not in the framework of Learning Studies (although there are some quasi-experimental, comparative studies, which very clearly demonstrate such differences; see Pang and Marton, 2003, 2004).

If this general improvement was one of the main results from our research, the other one was that "weaker students" improved more than others did (see Table 6.5 on p. 126 and Table 6.6 on p. 131) as far as the general level of achievement is concerned. But we can also observe specific effects within the various Learning Studies. Results from one of the cases offer an excellent example: in the very same Learning Study, students classified as "weaker students" improved much more than their classmates did. The "weaker students" started on a much lower level than the others did, but they caught up with and occasionally surpassed them. In fact, in 25 out of 27 Learning Studies, the weaker students showed significantly higher gains than did the high achievers (see Table 6.4 on p. 121). The adoption of more systematic ways of planning and carrying out the lesson obviously had a much stronger effect on students who were classified as academically less able. But why was that?

The explanation that the "weaker students" gained more from participating in Learning Studies — when measured by their appropriation of the object of learning — seems rather straightforward. A Learning Study starts with revealing what difficulties exist in a group of students as far as the mastering of a particular object of learning is concerned. It continues with creating the necessary conditions for bridging those difficulties. So, those who have them profit most from their difficulties being addressed.

This does not mean, however, that the only thing that is in a lesson is the necessary conditions for mastering a particular object of learning. It is only what has to be ascertained, which does not imply that it is the only thing that can be learnt. On pp. 122–3, we refer to some very interesting observations, to a case of unexpected learning, in which some students went beyond the object of learning and gained some insights in addition to mastering it. That means while some students learnt what they were expected to learn, other students — after having done so — learnt something more. How common this is should be an object of future investigations.

At this very moment, our conclusion is that focusing on the object of learning, learning from the learners, working with other teachers, using powerful theories, finding out how things work, is a good thing, we believe — for each and every one.

Our approach to learning and teaching in general and to individual differences in particular, originates from a specific perspective. Most learning theories take a psychological perspective, but Variation Theory starts with a pedagogical interest and espouses/assumes a pedagogical perspective. In consequence, teachers often find that it describes their experience better and that it is able to point the way for them more effectively than other theories do, and so they are attracted to it.

The theory challenges our assumptions about learning, and thus teaching. We regard different learning outcomes, not so much as a result of difference in ability but as a result of different perceptions. The fact that students do not learn what is intended is explained as not having seen or focused on the critical aspects required for a particular way of seeing intended by the teacher. This changes our approach to teaching. Teaching becomes a conscious structuring act, in which the teacher is supposed to mould learning experiences for students, to make it possible for them to discern the critical aspects required for understanding certain subject matter in a particular way, i.e., the object of learning.

We use the term object of learning instead of learning objectives. It is not just a change in terminology but also a change of attitude. Traditionally, the learning objectives are predetermined, by the curriculum, syllabus, or the teacher. In object of learning, we differentiate three types: the intended object of learning, the enacted object of learning, and the lived object of learning. By having the two terms "enacted" and "lived" object of learning, we formally acknowledge the fact that students do not always learn what is intended. What is enacted makes it possible for students to learn an object of learning, but what is lived depends on how each individual student experiences the lesson. By introducing V1, we give students a voice in determining the intended object of learning. This is not found simply by analysing the discipline but is negotiated by teachers, taking into account students' different ways of understanding. By recognizing the students as one of the stakeholders, genuine school-based curriculum development can take place.

Teachers often work in isolation, so that it is difficult for them to improve. In our case, teachers have the opportunity to observe each other teach the same content; the content is invariant, but the ways that different teachers deal with it differs, and student learning outcomes differ. Teachers then focus on the relationship between their teaching acts and student learning outcomes. Teachers seldom have the chance to observe other teachers teaching the same topic. By introducing V2, and a common language based on the conceptual framework, we are opening up opportunities for teachers to share their practice and to create learning communities in the schools.

Traditionally, the lesson is over at the end of the class, and the teacher has delivered and finished his or her duty. However, Learning Study encourages the teacher to take a research stance in teaching. Through cycles of the research lesson, teachers engage with planning the research lesson, gathering evidence and using this to feedback into their own teaching to improve student learning outcomes. Instead of trying to apply theory to practice, theory and practice become one. Teachers are researchers, helping to field test the Theory of Variation and making contributions to advance the theory, e.g., how patterns of variations can make it possible for students to appropriate various objects of learning and by doing so becoming more powerful participants in the future.

Appendix 1

The objects of learning and their critical aspects/features identified for the chosen topics during 2000–03:

Class	Topic	Object(s) of Learning	Critical Aspect(s)/Feature(s)
Mathematics			
2000–01			
P1	Contextualized problems of one-step addition and subtraction	The capability in using number facts to solve contextualized problems involving one-step	• Being familiar with the number facts, in particular the combinations of "3" and "4." • The meanings of the mathematical symbols involved, e.g., "+", "–" and "=". • The part-whole relationship embedded in an equation, e.g., "2 (part) + 3 (part) = 5 (whole)."
P1	Subtracting a single-digit number from a two-digit number smaller than 29	The capability in handling the problems by using regrouping strategies	Being familiar with the various ways of breaking ten into number facts, the smaller numbers.
P4	Comparing fractions	The understanding of the meaning and importance of "unit" in comparing fractions	Concepts of "equal share," "unit and unitizing," and part-whole comparison embedded in a fraction notation

(continued on p. 152)

(Appendix 1 continued)

Class	Topic	Object(s) of Learning	Critical Aspect(s)/ Feature(s)
P4	Area and perimeter	The understanding of the concepts involved in measuring the area and perimeter of a rectangle	Concepts involved in performing addition and multiplication to calculate for "perimeter" and "area" respectively; and the relationship between area and perimeter of the same rectangle.
2001–02			
P1	Contextualized problems of addition and subtraction	The capability in solving non-canonical types of problem	• The meanings of e.g., "+", "−" and the mathematical symbols involved, "=". • The part-whole relationship embedded in an equation, e.g., "2 (part) + 3 (part) = 5 (whole)."
P1	Reading time from clock face	The ability to read time from a clock face	The simultaneous movement of the two hands at different speeds.
P2	Quadrilaterals: features of rectangle and parallelogram	The understanding of • the features of rectangle • the features of parallelogram The capability in distinguishing these two types of quadrilateral	• The four interior angles in a rectangle are equal in "size" and they are called "right angles." • Opposite sides of a rectangle are equal in length and they are parallel to each other. • A parallelogram is a "squeezed" rectangle. • The major difference between parallelograms and rectangles: the former has two pairs of identical opposite angles, and the latter has all four angles equal.

(continued on p. 153)

(Appendix 1 continued)

Class	Topic	Object(s) of Learning	Critical Aspect(s)/ Feature(s)
Mathematics			
P2	Prisms (cylinders and right-angled prisms)	The understanding of the defining properties and structure of prisms	• There are two "tops" (or "upper surface and lower surface") on each prism. These two "tops" are identical in size and shape. • Prisms have "thickness." • The side edges of a prism are straight, equal in length, and parallel to each other. • A cylinder is a special case of the two "tops" being circles and there are no side edges.
P4	Comparing fractions	The understanding of the meaning and importance of "unit" in comparing fractions.	Concepts of "equal share," "unit and unitizing," and part-whole comparison embedded in a fraction notation.
P4	Quadrilaterals	The capability in distinguishing different types of quadrilateral (e.g., square-rhombus, rectangle-parallelogram)	• Basic concepts of "opposite angles," "right angles," "opposite sides," and "parallel lines." • Ways to measure the size of angles, length of sides, and whether two or more lines are parallel.
P5	Area of parallelogram	• The understanding of the concepts underlining the formula of the area of parallelogram • The ability to apply the formula	• Concepts of "base," "height," and their mutual perpendicularity. • Perpendicular distance as the shortest distance between a point and a line or between two parallel lines.

(continued on p. 154)

(Appendix 1 continued)

Class	Topic	Object(s) of Learning	Critical Aspect(s)/Feature(s)
P5	Volume of cube and cuboid	The understanding of • the concept of "volume" (versus capacity); • different ways in measuring volume (e.g., cube, cuboid, "H-shape," "E-shape.")	• Concept of "volume" as a three-dimensional measure of the amount of space that is enclosed within an object or solid shape. • Concepts involved in performing multiplication and/or addition/subtraction to calculate for the volume of an object.
2002–03			
P3	Triangles	The understanding of • what constitutes a triangle (basic features of a triangle); • what differentiates the three main types of triangle, i.e., right-angled triangles, isosceles triangles, and equilateral triangles (special features of each type of triangle)	• Every triangle has three angles and three sides (basic features). • Each of the three types of triangle is characterized by the length of the sides, the size of the angles, and the relation between the two (special features). • A sense of measuring for accuracy, and ways to measure the length of the sides and the size of the angles of a triangle.
Mathematics			
P6	Speed	The understanding of the concept of "speed" in the context of movements in the same direction.	• The concept of "proportion" underpinning the relationship between "distance" and "time" in determining "speed." • Two interrelationships between "time," "distance," and "speed," i.e., "Given the same time, the one who runs a longer distance is faster in speed;" and "Given the same distance, the one who runs in a shorter time is faster in speed."

(continued on p. 155)

(Appendix 1 continued)

Class	Topic	Object(s) of Learning	Critical Aspect(s)/Feature(s)
Chinese Language			
2000–01			
P4	讀文教學： 「一枝鉛筆頭」	• 能以不同動詞準確表達動作及以動詞短語表達情緒變化； • 掌握「拿、撿、接、丟、拋、掏、提」等近義詞在意義及運用上的微細分別。	• 適當地選擇動詞和副詞，對於利用說話及動作來表達人物不同程度的情緒，有很大影響。 • 不同語境下近義詞的運用。
P4	讀文教學： 「河邊的微笑」	• 了解不同修辭手法可以烘托感情； • 掌握文章的結構。	• 如何利用形容詞、對比等修辭手法，烘托作者對老師尊敬之情。 • 嚴謹的結構有助帶出文章的主題。 • 文中各段互相呼應以突顯作者對老師尊敬及懷念。
P4	新詩（格律）寫作	• 了解新詩的格律，如音節、押韻、鍊字等 • 能依格律寫作新詩。	• 音節和押韻可建構新詩的節奏感。 • 用字精鍊有助表現新詩的美感。 • 把散文精簡化使之產生節奏感而成為新詩。
2001–2002			
P4	新詩寫作—朗讀	掌握朗讀詩歌時的節奏感	• 押韻對朗讀詩歌的影響。 • 停頓、輕重與音節安排對朗讀詩歌的功能。
P4	閱讀策略	能夠綜合四種語文能力以提升閱讀的效能	綜合四種語文能力 • 聆聽：抓緊篇章的主題及重點； • 撰寫大綱：有效地從聆聽所得資料選出篇章的重點，並將之組織起來； • 複述：藉大綱複述文章的內容重點； • 評價：通過設問及分析以評估是否正確理解篇章內容。
Chinese Language			
P4	直述句和敘述句	能把直述句改寫成敘述句。	把直述句改寫成敘述句，改動的不單是格式（如標點），還包括人稱、語調、及內容上的相應變動。

(continued on p. 156)

(Appendix 1 continued)

Class	Topic	Object(s) of Learning	Critical Aspect(s)/ Feature(s)
P4	讀文教學：「鄭板橋」	能夠從選材的角度體會文章的深層意義。	文章中不同段落均選取了富代表性的技能或事件來突出主人翁的性格特點。
P5	讀文教學：「提高寫作能力的秘訣」	掌握文章的體裁—說明文。	首段提出了文章的主題；第二至四段各提出了一組例子以說明文章的主題；尾段為結語。
P5	明喻	• 掌握明喻句的結構及功能； • 懂得賞析及使用明喻法。	• 必須具備下列句子成分：本體、喻詞和喻體。 • 本體與喻體之間必須有共同/相通之處。 • 比喻的運用會使被描述的事物更豐富、更具體。 • 創作明喻句，學生必須運用想像／聯想力。
2002–03			
P6	比喻的欣賞和運用—以新詩為例	了解何謂準確及精采的比喻，並能在新詩寫作中加以運用。	• 準確：本體、喻體、喻解必須互相吻合。 • 精采：喻解豐富及別出心裁，而本體或喻體不一定是具體的物件，可以是抽象的事物。又可以多個喻體來比喻一個本體。
General Studies			
2001–02			
P3	The colour of light	The understanding of • the relationship between white light (or sunlight) and the rainbow; • three primary colours of light.	• The prism is only a tool used to split up the white light. • There is a direct relationship between white light and the rainbow. • All other colour lights can be formed by the three primary colours. • Primary colours cannot be formed by combination of other colour lights.

(continued on p. 157)

(Appendix 1 continued)

Class	Topic	Object(s) of Learning	Critical Aspect(s)/ Feature(s)
P3	Properties of water	The understanding of • the three states of water (gaseous, liquid, and solid) and the water cycle; • the concepts of "boiling" and "evaporation," and the difference between them.	• When water vapour meets cold surfaces, it will condense to become water droplets, which in turn will form ice when frozen. • Ice will melt into water when heated, and water will turn into water vapour when boiled or in the process of evaporation. • The concept that a gaseous state of water can be visible (when water is boiled) and invisible (water vapour in the air).
General Studies			
2002–03			
P4	Closed circuits	• The understanding of the flow of an electric current in a closed circuit; • Awareness of the safety in the use of electricity.	• In a closed circuit, electricity is able to move round the circuit without any gap • A battery (as a force of propulsion) is needed for an electric current to flow • Electricity is not used up in a circuit. • The quantity of electric current varies and can be dangerous when it is large.
P4	Price	• The understanding of the way of conceiving "price" in economics	• The importance of both demand and supply factors on "price"

(continued on p. 158)

(Appendix 1 continued)

Class	Topic	Object(s) of Learning	Critical Aspect(s)/ Feature(s)
English Language			
2002–03			
P4	Subject-verb agreement in simple present tense	The capability to conform to subject-verb agreement in simple present tense in talking about professions	The addition of "s/es" to the verb form under the following conditions: • the subject item being third person singular; • present tense.

Appendix 2

A summary of the seminars/ workshops/ conferences members took part in during the academic years 2000–01, 2001–02 and 2002–03.

Seminars and workshops given to the project schools 於伙伴學校舉辦的研討會及工作坊	
Date 日期	**Function (Organizer)** 活動（主辦機構）
2000/1/24	照顧學生個別差異—「差異」開始　工作坊（一、二）（學校一）
2000/2/14	照顧學生個別差異—「差異」開始　工作坊（一）（學校二）
2000/2/18	照顧學生個別差異—「差異」開始　工作坊（三）（學校一）
2000/4/28	照顧學生個別差異—「差異」開始　工作坊（二）（學校二）
2000/5/18	照顧學生個別差異—「差異」開始　工作坊（四）（學校一）
2000/6/2	照顧學生個別差異—「差異」開始　工作坊（三）（學校二）
2000/6/30	照顧學生個別差異—「差異」開始　工作坊（四）（學校二）
2001/8/24	個別差異研究計畫第一年檢討及第二年前瞻 (學校一)
2002/3/27	研究課的經驗分享與及同儕觀課的技巧 (學校一)
2002/4/25	照顧學生個別差異—「差異」開始研究計畫：回顧與前瞻 (學校三)
Public seminars and workshops 公開的研討會和工作坊	
Date 日期	**Function (Organizer)** 活動（主辦機構）
2000/4/23	School recruitment seminar (CDI, HKSAR)
2000/10/28	Catering for Individual Learning Differences (Primary Education) Seminar Series (CDI, HKSAR)
2000/12/21	研究課與課堂分析 (課程發展處)
2001/3/15	個別差異研究研討會系列（一）第一場 (課程發展處)
2001/3/31	個別差異研究研討會系列（一）第二場 (課程發展處)
2001/5/17	A lesson study — Unit and Unitizing (CDI, HKSAR)
2001/11/7	個別差異研究研討會系列（二）（課程發展署)

(continued on p. 160)

(Appendix 2 continued)

2002/1/23	Lesson Study as a tool to improve teaching and learning (CDSPFE, HKIEd)
2002/2/6	如何利用「課堂學習研究」提升教學質素 (香港教育學院院校協作中心)
2002/2/27	小四數學研究課：面積和周界 (香港教育學院院校協作中心)
2002/3/6	小三常識研究課：光的顏色　第一場 (香港教育學院院校協作中心)
2002/4/9	小四中文研究課：直述句和敍述句 (香港教育學院院校協作中心)
2002/4/13	Workshop for HKIEd Honorary Teacher Advisors　(CDSPFE, HKIED)
2002/4/20	Workshop for HKIEd Honorary Teacher Advisors　(CDSPFE, HKIED)
2002/4/20	小三常識研究課：光的顏色　第二場 (香港教育學院院校協作中心)
2002/5/4	小四中文研究課：新詩寫作 (香港教育學院院校協作中心)
2002/5/11	照顧學生個別差異—「差異」開始 (新界西教區聯校研討會)
2002/5/11	照顧學生個別差異—「差異」開始研究計畫 (澳門大學附屬小學)
2002/5/25	小一及小四數學研究課：破十法及分數 (香港教學院院校協作中心)
2002/6/29	個別差異研討會：照顧學生個別差異—「差異」開始研究計畫 (課程發展處)
2002/10/28	如何利用學生的學習差異設計有效的教學流程 (保良局董玉娣中學)
2002/11/12	照顧個別差異—「差異」開始 (「學會學習」薈萃 02，教育署)
2002/11/27	課堂學習研究：透過教師專業發展以照顧學生學習差異 (第一場) (課程發展處及香港教育學院院校協作中心)
2002/12/14	小四數學課堂學習研究：分數的單位與單位化 (香港教育學院院校協作中心)
2003/1/22	課堂學習研究：透過教師專業發展以照顧學生學習差異 (第二場) (課程發展處及香港教育學院院校協作中心)
2003/1/29	課堂學習研究系列：小三常識「光的顏色」(課程發展處及香港教育學院院校協作中心)
2003/2/15	課堂學習研究系列：小四數學「面積與周界」(課程發展處及香港教育學院院校協作中心)
2003/2/22	課堂學習研究系列：小四中文「新詩（一）」(課程發展處及香港教育學院院校協作中心)
2003/3/8	課堂學習研究系列：小三常識「水」(香港教育學院院校協作中心及地區教師專業發展交流計畫)
2003/5/7	課堂學習研究系列：小五數學「體積」(香港教育學院院校協作中心)
2003/5/10	課堂學習研究系列：小四中文「一枝鉛筆頭」(香港教育學院院校協作中心)
2003/6/28	課堂學習研究系列：小四中文「新詩（二）」(香港教育學院院校協作中心)
2003/11/12	「拓寬學習空間」知識薈萃 2003　(教育統籌局)
2003/12/1	Catering for Individual Differences — Building on Variation (CDI, HKSAR)

(continued on p. 161)

(Appendix 2 continued)

Local and international conferences 於本地與海外舉行的研討會議	
Date 日期	**Function (Organizer)** 活動（主辦機構）
2000/12/9	Departmental Conference 2000 at Gold Coast (Former Department of Curriculum Studies, HKU)
2001/6/30	A lesson study — P1 Math on 'breaking a ten' (UPDP, HKU)
2001/9/1	Variation in practice (EARLI' 2001)
2002/4/25	Lesson Study / Analysis: Chinese Language (UPD Fellowship Programme on Mentoring, UPDP, Faculty of Education, HKU)
2003/8/28	Pattern of variation in teaching the colour of light (EARLI 2003)
2003/10/25	〈建構與擬寫提綱的課堂研究—語文綜合能力的轉換中介〉，第七屆現代應用文國際研討會（香港大學教育學院母語教學支援中心）。

Appendix 3

List of Publications on "Catering for Individual Differences—Building on Variation"

Conference papers

1. Lo, M. L. (2001). Variation in Practice — The effects of a 'research lesson' on a group of Chinese language teachers and their pupils, *9th European Conference for Research on Learning and Instruction* (September 2001).
2. Lo, M. L., Chik, P. M. & Pang, M. F. (2003). Patterns of variation in teaching the colour of light to primary three students. Symposium presentation, *10th European Conference for Research on Learning and Instruction* (August 2003).
3. Pong, W. Y. (2001). Making Conscious Use of Variation, *9th European Conference for Research on Learning and Instruction* (September 2001).
4. 吳鳳平、林偉業 (2003)。〈建構與擬寫提綱的課堂研究 —— 語文綜合能力的轉換中介〉，第七屆現代應用文國際研討會，香港大學教育學院母語教學支援中心。

Books/ Chapters/ Journal papers/ Newspaper articles

5. Lo, M. L., Pong, W. Y., Marton, F., Leung, A. Y. L., Ko, P. K., Ng, F. P., Pang, M. F., Chik, P. P. M., Chan, F. S. S. & Tang, A. A. C. (2002). *Catering for Individual Differences — Building on Variation (The first findings).* Hong Kong: INSTEP, Faculty of Education, The University of Hong Kong.
6. Lo, M. L., Marton, F., Ng, F. P., Ko, P. K., Mok, I. A. C., Wong, K. M., Pang, M. F., Pong, W. Y., Morris, P., Runesson, U., Chik, P. P. M. Luk, A. S. L. (2000) *Catering for Individual Differences — Building on Variation: Teacher Training and Self-learning CD Package (Chinese version).* Hong Kong: Hong Kong Government Printer.
7. Marton, F. & Morris, P. (Eds.) (2002). *What matters? Discovering critical conditions of classroom learning.* Göteborg: Acta Universitatis Gothoburgensis.
8. Marton, F. & Tsui, A. B. M. with Chik, P. P. M. , Ko, P. Y., Lo, M. L., Mok, I. A. C., Ng, F. P., Pang, M. F., Pong, W. Y., and Runesson, U. (2004). *Classroom discourse and the space of learning,* New Jersey: Lawrence Erlbaum Associates, Inc., Publishers.
9. 盧敏玲 (2005)。「課堂學習研究」對香港教育的影響，＜開放教育研究＞。
10. 盧敏玲、高寶玉 (2004)。提高教學的質素 —— 課堂學習研究的理論與實踐，＜亞太語文教育學報＞。
11. 盧敏玲、龐永欣、馬飛龍、梁玉麟、高寶玉、吳鳳平、植佩敏 (2001)。＜個別差異發展及研究報告系列：照顧個別差異 —— 從「差異」開始＞，香港：政府印務局。
12. 龐永欣、聖愛德華天主教小學小一數學組 (2002)。＜閱讀鐘面的時間：時正、時半＞，明報教得樂，2002年4月30日。

Unpublished theses

12. MEd. (2002) 鍾淑芬，《小學新詩音節教學課堂個案分析》，香港大學教育學院。
13. BEd. (2002) 林海山，《從仿作到創作 —— 新詩教學課堂的話語分析》，香港大學教育學院。
14. BEd. (2003) 袁詠儀，《指令語言與教學活動的成效 —— 閱讀策略訓練課堂語言分析》，香港大學教育學院。

Appendix 4

Appendix 4.1

The detailed information and statistical results of the comparisons of the gain score of the whole group in each of the 27 Learning Studies conducted during the academic years 2000–01, 2001–02, and 2002–03.

Subject (Level — no. of Learning Study)	No. of participants	Mean score (full mark scaled to 100) Whole group				
		Pre-test	Post-test	Gain score (post-test minus pre-test)	Significance level of the change (one-tailed paired *t*-test, p<0.05)	
					p-value	t-value
2000–01, School 1						
Math (P1: 1st)	168	40.06	79.23	39.17	0.00*	18.76
Math (P4)	151	58.20	70.20	11.99	0.00*	13.83
Math (P1: 2nd)	151	80.23	88.65	8.41	0.00*	6.48
2000–01, School 2						
Chin (P4: 1st)	144	62.60	80.99	18.39	0.00*	14.35
Chin (P4: 2nd)	150	21.22	22.06	0.84	0.11	1.26
Chin (P4: 3rd)	154	26.46	44.72	18.26	0.00*	11.92
2001–02, School 1						
Math (P1: 1st)	150	43.27	67.11	23.83	0.00*	9.33
Math (P2: 1st)	144	46.20	51.46	5.26	0.00	3.25
Math (P4: 1st)	198	52.19	56.29	4.10	0.00*	5.14
Chin (P4: 1st)	198	36.93	62.24	25.31	0.00*	21.10
Math (P5: 1st)	135	73.47	75.84	2.37	0.10	1.30
Math (P1: 2nd)	163	66.67	92.18	25.52	0.00*	16.92
Math (P2: 2nd)	182	22.12	53.30	31.18	0.00*	19.64
Math (P4: 2nd)	200	22.88	54.73	31.85	0.00*	26.12
Math (P5: 2nd)	168	63.65	70.04	6.39	0.00*	5.68

(continued on p. 165)

(Appendix 4.1 continued)

2001–02, School 2					
GS (P3: 1st)	106	24.91	56.13	31.23	0.00*	14.11
Chin (P4: 1st)	127	25.75	55.75	30.00	0.00*	18.10
Chin (P5: 1st)	163	42.59	50.57	7.98	0.00*	4.63
GS (P3: 2nd)	100	43.83	74.80	30.97	0.00*	9.53
Chin (P4: 2nd)	125	52.34	54.69	2.34	0.11	1.24
Chin (P5: 2nd)	156	61.43	66.33	4.89	0.00	3.72
2002–03, School 1					
Math (P3)	173	57.12	68.55	11.43	0.00*	9.93
Math (P6)	169	39.24	46.38	7.14	0.00*	10.10
GS (P4)	160	48.67	68.92	20.25	0.00*	7.51
2002–03, School 2					
GS (P4)	91	16.00	46.40	30.40	0.00*	10.48
Eng (P4)	72	47.32	64.58	17.26	0.00*	4.30
Chin (P6)	149	34.46	40.38	5.92	0.00*	5.04

* The numeric value is nearest to zero (as distinguished from those equal to zero).

Appendix 4.2

The detailed information and statistical results of the comparisons of the gain score of the high-score group in each of the 27 Learning Studies conducted during the academic years 2000–01, 2001–02, and 2002–03.

Subject (Level — no. of Learning Study)	No. of participants	Mean score (full mark scaled to 100)				
		High-score group				
		Pre-test	Post-test	Gain score (post-test minus pre-test)	Significance level of the change (1-tailed paired *t*-test, p<0.05)	
					p-value	*t*-value
2000–01, School 1						
Math (P1: 1st)	44	68.41	80.45	12.04	0.00	3.49
Math (P4)	56	73.28	83.66	10.38	0.00*	10.03
Math (P1: 2nd)	43	96.12	94.93	-1.19	0.17	0.97
2000–01, School 2						
Chin (P4: 1st)	64	76.93	91.44	14.51	0.00*	13.32
Chin (P4: 2nd)	49	34.51	34.27	-0.24	0.42	-0.21
Chin (P4: 3rd)	51	41.42	56.86	15.44	0.00*	7.29
2001–02, School 1						
Math (P1: 1st)	69	57.97	71.38	13.41	0.00	3.73
Math (P2: 1st)	46	62.82	52.75	-10.07	0.00	-3.30
Math (P4: 1st)	51	72.55	75.10	2.55	0.04	1.78
Chin (P4: 1st)	55	52.49	77.11	24.62	0.00*	14.15
Math (P5:1st)	62	83.33	77.69	-5.64	0.02	-2.06

(continued on p. 166)

(Appendix 4.2 continued)

Math (P1: 2nd)	63	84.13	95.77	11.64	0.00*	10.00
Math (P2: 2nd)	96	33.72	58.85	25.13	0.00*	11.88
Math (P4: 2nd)	67	41.79	74.74	32.95	0.00*	16.57
Math (P5: 2nd)	44	87.35	87.65	0.30	0.39	0.28
2001–02, School 2						
GS (P3: 1st)	43	38.84	63.49	24.65	0.00*	6.54
Chin (P4: 1st)	38	46.58	45.00	-1.58	0.32	-0.46
Chin (P5: 1st)	59	62.47	57.38	-5.09	0.02	-2.13
GS (P3: 2nd)	25	60.00	77.14	17.14	0.00*	4.81
Chin (P4: 2nd)	54	73.46	66.98	-6.48	0.01	-2.62
Chin (P5: 2nd)	45	84.89	81.93	-2.96	0.04	-1.84
2002–03, School 1						
Math (P3)	52	71.26	74.79	3.53	0.02	2.18
Math (P6)	44	57.29	59.56	2.27	0.02	2.06
GS (P4)	108	66.67	73.46	6.79	0.00	3.78
2002–03, School 2						
GS (P4)	51	21.18	36.08	14.90	0.00*	5.57
Eng (P4)	26	70.60	65.66	-4.94	0.18	-0.94
Chin (P6)	39	50.27	49.12	-1.15	0.25	-0.69

* The numeric value is nearest to zero (as distinguished from those equal to zero).

Appendix 4.3

The detailed information and statistical results of the comparisons of the gain score of the low-score group in each of the 27 Learning Studies conducted during the academic years 2000–01, 2001–02, and 2002–03.

Subject (level — no. of Learning Study)	No. of participants	Mean score (with full mark scaled to 100)				Improved score (post-test minus pre-test)	
		Low-score group					
		Pre-test	Post-test	Gain score (post-test minus pre-test)	Significance level of the change (1-tailed paired *t*-test, p<0.05)	Significance level of the difference between low-score and high-score groups (1-tailed 2-sample equal variance *t*-test, p<0.05)	
					p-value	t-value	p-value	t-value
2000–01, School 1							
Math (P1:1st)	77	21.04	76.49	55.45	0.00*	24.05	0.00*	10.46
Math (P4)	42	39.07	53.26	14.19	0.00*	7.00	0.05	1.68
Math (P1: 2nd)	43	49.61	75.97	26.36	0.00*	9.08	0.00*	8.73

(continued on p. 167)

(Appendix 4.3 continued)

2000–01, School 2								
Chin (P4: 1st)	40	41.07	65.12	24.05	0.00*	7.42	0.00	2.79
Chin (P4: 2nd)	44	6.75	9.56	2.81	0.01	2.35	0.03	1.86
Chin (P4: 3rd)	40	9.69	24.38	14.69	0.00	4.04	0.43	-0.18
2001–02, School 1								
Math (P1: 1st)	81	16.05	58.02	41.97	0.00*	13.54	0.00*	6.02
Math (P2: 1st)	47	31.47	47.03	15.56	0.00*	7.64	0.00*	6.98
Math (P4: 1st)	50	31.15	37.21	6.06	0.00	3.47	0.07	1.51
Chin (P4: 1st)	54	22.53	41.38	18.85	0.00*	7.46	0.03	-1.88
Math (P5: 1st)	34	36.76	58.82	22.06	0.00*	5.75	0.00*	5.29
Math (P1: 2nd)	61	43.72	86.16	42.44	0.00*	17.27	0.00*	11.33
Math (P2: 2nd)	86	9.16	47.09	37.93	0.00*	17.38	0.00*	4.21
Math (P4: 2nd)	51	4.98	32.13	27.15	0.00*	11.26	0.03	-26.12
Math (P5: 2nd)	44	32.35	47.42	15.07	0.00*	5.09	0.00*	4.69
2001–02, School 2								
GS (P3: 1st)	63	15.40	51.11	35.71	0.00*	13.75	0.01	2.42
Chin (P4: 1st)	40	6.00	69.00	63.00	0.00*	19.65	0.00*	13.76
Chin (P5: 1st)	52	19.78	42.31	22.53	0.00*	6.95	0.00*	6.86
GS (P3: 2nd)	45	15.56	41.73	26.17	0.00*	7.68	0.00*	-10.03
Chin (P4: 2nd)	38	20.61	34.65	14.04	0.00	3.86	0.00*	4.66
Chin (P5: 2nd)	44	32.00	45.93	13.93	0.00*	5.75	0.00*	5.68
2002–03, School 1								
Math (P3)	61	42.99	63.93	20.94	0.00*	10.51	0.00*	6.79
Math (P6)	52	20.89	28.85	7.96	0.00*	5.48	0.00	-10.10
GS (P4)	52	8.33	61.54	53.21	0.00*	11.80	0.00*	9.56
2002–03, School 2								
GS (P4)	38	0.00	47.80	47.80	0.00*	12.01	0.00*	5.39
Eng (P4)	27	19.31	69.84	50.53	0.00*	7.96	0.00*	6.43
Chin (P6)	39	17.41	32.05	14.64	0.00*	5.65	0.00*	5.13

* The numeric value is nearest to zero (as distinguished from those equal to zero).

References

Bassey, M. (1999). *Case study research in educational setting.* Philadelphia, PA: Open University Press.

Bereiter, C. and Scardamalia, M. (1993). *Surpassing ourselves: an inquiry into nature and implications of expertise.* Chicago, IL: Open Court.

Bowden, J. and Marton, F. (1998). *The university of learning.* London: Kogan Page.

Bransford, J. D., Brown, A. B., and Cocking, R. R. (Eds.) (2002). *How people learn: brain, mind, experience, and school.* Washington, DC: National Academy Press.

Brentano, F. (1874). *Psychology from an empirical standpoint.* London: Routledge and Kegan Paul.

Brophy, J. (Ed.) (1992). *Advances in research on teaching, Vol. 3. Planning and managing learning tasks and activities.* London: JAI Press.

Chik, P. P. M. and Lo, M. L. (2004). Simultaneity and the enacted object of learning. In F. Marton and A. B. M. Tsui (Eds.) *Classroom discourse and the space of learning.* Mahwah, NJ: Lawrence Erlbaum Associates, Inc., Publishers.

Chinn, C. A. and Brewer, W. F. (1993). The role of anomalous data in knowledge acquisition: A theoretical framework and implications for science instruction. *Review of Educational Research, 63*, pp. 1–49.

Clement, J. (1982). Students' preconceptions in introductory mechanics, *American Journal of Physics, 50(1),* pp. 66–71.

Clement, J. (1983). A conceptual model discussed by Galileo and used intuitively by physics students. In D. Gentner and A. Stevens (Eds.) *Mental models.* Hillsdale, NJ: Erlbaum.

Cochran-Smith, M. and Lytle, S. L. (2001). Beyond certainty: Taking an inquiry stance on practice. In A. Lieberman and L. Miller (Eds.) *Teachers caught in the action: Professional development that matters.* NY: Teachers College Press, pp. 45–58.

Cohen, L. and Manion, L. (1994). *Research methods in education.* London: Routledge.

Confrey, J. (1990). A review of research on student conceptions in mathematics, science and programming. *Review of Research in Education, 16*, pp. 3–56.

Connelly, M. and Clandinin, D. J. (1995). Teachers' professional knowledge landscapes: Secret, sacred, and cover stories. In D. J. Clandinin and M. Connelly (Eds.) *Teachers' professional knowledge landscapes.* New York and London: Columbia University, Teachers College Press, pp. 3–15.

Csikszentmihayi, I. S. (Ed.) (1988). *Optimal experience: psychological studies of flow in consciousness.* Cambridge: Cambridge University Press.

Cuban, L. (1990). Reforming again, again, and again, *Educational Researcher, 19(1)*, pp. 3–13.

Curriculum Development Council (2002). *General studies for primary schools curriculum guide*. HKSAR: Education Department, HKSAR Government.

Dahlgren, L. O. (1978). *Effects of university education on the conception of reality*. Reports from the Institute of Education, University of Göteborg.

Dahlgren, L. O. (1979). *Children's conception of price as a function of questions asked (81)*. Göteborg: Institute of Education, University of Göteborg.

Doyle, W. (1983). Academic work. *Review of Educational Research, 53*, pp. 159–99.

Doyle, W. (1986). Content representation in teachers' definitions of academic work. *Journal of Curriculum Studies, 18*, pp. 365–79.

Duit, R. and Treagust, D. F. (1995). Students' conceptions and constructivist teaching approaches. In B. J. Fraser and H. J. Walberg (Eds.) *Improving science education*. Chicago, IL: The National Society For The Study Of Education.

Elbaz, F. (1983). *Teacher thinking: A study of practical knowledge*. London: Croom Helm.

Entwistle, N. (1984). Contrasting perspectives on learning. In F. Marton, D. Hounsell, and N. Entwistle (Eds.) *The experience of learning*. Edinburgh: Scottish Academic Press.

Gardner, H. (1984). The development of competence in culturally defined domains. In R. Shweder and R. LeVine (Eds.) *Culture theory: Essays of mind, self and emotion*. Cambridge: Cambridge University Press.

Gardner, H. (1991). *The unschooled mind*. New York: BasicBooks.

Gu, L.Y. (1991). *Xuehui Jiaoxue (Learning to teach)*. Hubei: People's Press.

Hattie, J. (1999). *Influences on student learning*. Inaugural lecture: Professor of Education, University of Auckland (August).

Hounsell, D. (1984). Learning and essay-writing. In F. Marton, D. Hounsell, and N. Entwistle (Eds.) *The experience of learning*. Edinburgh: Scottish Academic Press.

Johansson, B., Marton, F., and Svensson, L. (1985). An approach to describing learning as a change between qualitatively different conceptions. In A.L. Pines and T.H. West (Eds.) *Cognitive structure and conceptual change*. New York: Academic Press.

Koumaras, P. Kariotoglou, P. and Psillos, D. (1997). Causal structures and counter intuitive experiments in electricity, *International Journal of Science Education, 9*, pp. 617–30.

Lamon, S. J. (1999). *Teaching fractions and ratios for understanding: Essential content knowledge and instructional strategies for teachers*. Mahwah, NJ: Lawrence Erlbaum Associates, Publishers.

Laurillard, D. (1995). *Understanding representations*. Paper presented at the symposium Understanding Understanding II, Edinburg, Scotland (May, 1995).

Lave, J. (1996). Teaching as learning, in practice. *Mind, Culture, and Activity, 3, 3*, pp. 149–64.

Lieberman, A. and Miller, L. (Eds.) (2001). *Teachers caught in the action: Professional development that matters*. NY: Teachers College Press.

Lincoln, Y. S. and Guba, E. G. (1985). *Naturalistic inquiry*. Newbury Park, CA: Sage Publications.

Little, J.W. (2001). Professional development in pursuit of school reform. In A. Lieberman and L. Miller (Eds.) *Teachers caught in the action: Professional development that matters*, pp. 23–44. New York: Teachers College Press.

Lo, M. L. and Ko, P. Y. (2002). The "enacted" object of learning. In F. Marton and P. Morris (Eds.) *What matters?Discovering critical conditions of classroom learning.* Göteborg: Acta Universitatis Gothoburgensis.

Lo, M. L., Marton, F., Pang, M. F., and Pong, W. Y. (2004). Towards a pedagogy of learning. In F. Marton and A. B. M. Tsui (Eds.) *Classroom discourse and the space of learning.* Mahwah, NJ: Lawrence Erlbaum Associates, Inc., Publishers.

Lortie, D. (1975). *Schoolteacher.* Chicago, IL: University of Chicago Press.

Ma, L. P. (1999). *Knowing and teaching elementary mathematics: Teachers' understanding of fundamental mathematics in China and the United States.* Mahwah, NJ: Lawrence Erlbaum Associates.

Marton, F. (2001). *The Learning Study.* Unpublished manuscript.

Marton, F. and Booth, S. (1997). *Learning and awareness.* Mahwah, NJ: Lawrence Erlbaum Associates.

Marton, F. and Morris, P. (Eds.) (2002). *What matters? Discovering critical conditions of classroom learning.* Göteborg: Acta Universitatis Gothoburgensis.

Marton, F. and Pang, M. F. (2004). *On some necessary conditions of learning.* The Manuscript.

Marton, F. and Runesson, U. (2003). The space of learning. Paper presented at the symposium *Improving Learning, Fostering the will to learn, European Association for Research on Learning and Instruction,* Padova, Italy (August, 2003).

Marton, F. and Säljö, R. (1976) On qualitative differences in learning I: Outcome and process. *British Journal of Educational Psychology, 46,* pp. 4–11.

Marton, F. and Tsui, A. B. M. with Chik, P. P. M., Ko, P. Y., Lo, M. L., Mok, I. A. C., Ng, F. P., Pang, M. F., Pong, W. Y. and Runesson, U. (2004). *Classroom discourse and the space of learning.* Mahwah, NJ: Lawrence Erlbaum Associates, Inc., Publishers.

Marton, F. (1977) Människors mottagande och användning av information. In B. Fjaestad (Ed.) *Lyssna, titta, läsa. Rapport från ett symposium om kommunikationsteknologi och perception.* Stockholm: Riksbankens Jubileumsfond, 2, pp. 47–50.

Marton, F., Beaty, E., and Dall'Alba, G. (1993). Conceptions of learning, *International Journal of Educational Research, 19,* pp. 277–300.

Mercer, N. (Ed.) (2000). *Words and minds.* London: Routledge.

Metioui, A., Brassard, C., Levasseur, F. and Lavoie, M. (1996). The persistence of students' unfolded beliefs about electrical circuits: The case of Ohm's law, *International Journal of Science Education, 18,* pp. 193–212.

Miller, G. A. (1956). The magic number seven, plus or minus two. Some limits on our capacity to process information, *Psychological Review, 63,* pp. 81–7.

Morris, P. (2000). The commissioning and decommissioning of curriculum reforms — the career of the target-oriented curriculum. In B. Adamson, T. Kwan and K. K. Chan (Eds.) *Changing the curriculum: The impact of reform on primary schooling in Hong Kong.* Hong Kong: Hong Kong University Press.

Neuman, D. (1987). *The origin of arithmetic skills: A phenomenographic approach.* Göteborg: Acta Universitatis Gothoburgensis.

Nussbaum, J. (1985). Children's conception of the earth as a cosmic body. In R. Driver, E. Guesne, and A. Tiberghien (Eds.) *Children's ideas in Science.* Buckingham: Open University Press.

Pang, M. F. and Marton, F. (2003). Beyond "lesson study" — Comparing two ways of facilitating the grasp of economic concepts, *Instructional Science, 31(3),* pp. 175–94.

Pang, M. F. (2002). *Making learning possible: the use of variation in the teaching of school economics.* PhD Thesis. Hong Kong: University of Hong Kong.

Pang, M. F. (2003). Two faces of Variation — On continuity in the phenomenographic movement, *Scandinavian Journal of Educational Research, 47(2)*, pp. 145–56.

Pardhan, H. and Bano, Y. (2001). Science teachers' alternate conceptions about direct-currents, *International Journal of Science Education, 23*, pp. 301–18.

Pong, W. Y. and Morris, P. (2002). Accounting for differences in achievement. In F. Marton and P. Morris (Eds.) *What matters? Discovering critical conditions of classroom learning.* Göteborg: Acta Universitatis Gothoburgensis.

Pong, W. Y. (2000). *Widening the Space of Variation — Inter-contextual and Intra-contextual Shifts in Pupils' Understanding of Two Economic Concepts.* PhD Thesis. Hong Kong: University of Hong Kong.

Resnick, L. B., Levine, J. M. and Teasley, S. D. (Eds.) (1991). *Perspectives on socially shared cognition.* Washington, DC: American Psychological Association.

Säljö, R. (1975). *Qualitative differences in learning as a function of the learner's conception of the task.* Göteborg: Acta Univertsitatis Gothoburgensis

Säljö, R. (1982). *Learning and understanding: A study of differences in constructing meaning from a text.* Göteborg: Acta Universitatis Gothoburgensis.

Säljö, R. (1996). Mental and physical artifacts in cognitive processes. In P. Reinman and H. Spanda (Eds.) *Learning in humans and machines: towards an interdisciplinary learning science,* pp. 83–96. New York: Pergamon Press.

Shipstone, D. (1993). Electricity in simple circuits. In R. Driver, E. Gusene and A. Tiberghien (Eds.) *Children's ideas in science.* Buckingham: Open University Press.

Shulman, L. (1986). Those who understand: Knowledge growth in teaching. *Educational Researcher, 15(2)*, 4–14.

Sipe, T. A. and Curlette, W. L. (1997). A meta-synthesis of factors related to educational achievement: A methodological approach to summarizing the synthesizing meta-analyses, *International Journal of Educational Research, 25*, pp. 583–698.

Skemp, R. R. (1971). *The psychology of learning mathematics.* London: Penguin Books Ltd.

Solomon, D. and Kendall, A.J. (1979). *Children in classrooms: An investigation of person-environment interaction.* New York: Praeger.

Stigler, J. W. and Hiebert, J. (1999). *The teaching gap.* New York: The Free Press.

Tasker, R. and Osborne, R. (1990). Science teaching and science learning. In R. Osborne and P. Freyberg (Eds.) *Learning in science project: The implication of children's science.* Hong Kong: Heinemann.

Thomas, L. M. (1983). *12–16-year-old Pupils' Understanding of Economics.* Unpublished PhD Thesis. London: University of London.

Tyack, D. and Cuban, L. (1995). *Tinkering toward utopia: A century of public school reform.* Cambridge, MA: Harvard University Press.

Vosniadou, S. and Brewer, W. F. (1992). Mental models of the earth: A study of conceptual change in childhood. *Cognitive Psychology, 24*, pp. 535–85.

Vosniadou, S. and Brewer, W. F. (1990). A cross-cultural investigation of children's conceptions about the Earth, the Sun and the Moon: Greek and American data. In H. Mandl, E. De Corte, N. Bennett and H. F. Friedrid (Eds.) *Learning and instruction. European Research in an International Context, 2.2.* Oxford: Pergamon Press, pp. 605–29.

Vosniadou, S. and Brewer, W. F. (1987). Theories of knowledge restructuring in development. *Review of Educational Research, 57*, pp. 51–67.

Vosniadou, S., and Brewer, W. F. (1994). Mental models of the day/night cycle. *Cognitive Science, 18*, pp. 123–83.

Wang, M. C., Walberg, H. J. and Haertel, G. D. (1993). Toward a knowledge base: Why, how, for whom? *Review of Educational Research, 63*, pp. 365–76.

Werner, H. (1980). Fachdidaktik aus der Sicht des Fachdidaktikers. In D. Rodi and W. Bauer (Hrsg) Biologiedidaktik als Wissenschaft. Köln. Aulis. S.61–85Yin, R. K. (1994). *Case study research, design and methods.* London: Sage.

盧敏玲、高寶玉 (2003)。〈提高中國語文教學的質素：課堂學習研究的理論與實踐〉，《亞太語文教育學報第六卷第一期》。香港：香港教育學院語文教育中心，頁21–43。

Index